IMAGES
of America

R.E. OLDS AND
INDUSTRIAL LANSING

GROUND BREAKING FOR OLDS TOWER, 1930. Pictured is R.E. Olds, Lansing Industrial pioneer.

Cover: **CURVED DASH OLDSMOBILE, 1903.** In one of the many early publicity stunts for the new horseless carriage, Olds Motor Works climbed the steps of Lansing's Capitol building to demonstrate the power and versatility of the new machine.

IMAGES
of America

R.E. Olds and
Industrial Lansing

Michael Rodriguez

ARCADIA

Published by Arcadia Publishing,
an imprint of Tempus Publishing, Inc.
Charleston SC, Chicago, Portsmouth NH,
San Francisco

Printed in Great Britain.

Library of Congress Catalog Card Number: 2004102269

For all general information contact Arcadia Publishing at:
Telephone 843-853-2070
Fax 843-853-0044
E-Mail sales@arcadiapublishing.com
For customer service and orders:
Toll-Free 1-888-313-2665

Visit us on the internet at http://www.arcadiapublishing.com

CONTENTS

ACKNOWLEDGMENTS

Thank you to the volunteers at the R.E. Olds Transportation Museum, and especially to David Pfaff for his assistance and research. Thank you to the staff at the Walter P. Reuther Library, especially Elizabeth Clemens. Also thanks to everyone at the Michigan State University Library for their continued support, and to the MSU Archives and Historical Collections. Very large thanks to Jim MacLean at the Capital Area District Library Local History Room, whose generous assistance made this book possible.

Photo Credits:
Forest Parke Memorial Library/ Capital Area District Library (FPML/CADL.)
David R. Caterino Collection/ Capital Area District Library (Caterino/CADL.)
R.E. Olds Transportation Museum (REOTM.)
Oldsmobile History Center (OHC.)
Michigan State University Archives and Historical Collections (MSUAHC.)
Walter P. Reuther Library, Wayne State University (Reuther.)
Gladys Olds Anderson (see Bibliography)
Henry B. Baker (see Bibliography)

INTRODUCTION

"Mark the spirit of invention everywhere, thy rapid patents,
Thy continual workshops, foundries, risen or rising,
See, from their chimneys how the tall flame-fires stream."
—from *Song of the Exposition*, Walt Whitman

When Walt Whitman wrote about what he considered the greatness of American industry, after the close of the Civil War and just before the Columbian Exposition, he was a poet excited by the potential of a country poised to be the manufacturing capital of the world. In 1871, America was a country struggling through reconstruction and was finding its identity and geographical balance through the building of its cities and the making of its machines. Between 1830 and 1880 the population of the U.S. had increased by 400 percent, and a full 22 percent of that total were then living in urban areas. The agrarian way of life in was disappearing into America's past. Lansing was made within this atmosphere. The city emerged from a dense forest previously thought uninhabitable and became a new industrial center and hub of state government surrounded by farming communities—and this geographic and economic transformation happened within a span of 50-odd years.

The development of Lansing is an interesting study of the tension between the farm and the factory. Without the factory life and the close-knit proximity of workers, it would have had to rely solely on the arrival of the new government for the development of its infrastructure, its tax base, and its cosmopolitan center. And, ironically enough, what the factories of the city produced in greatest quantity between 1870 and 1900 were agricultural tools for the settling of the West. The early inhabitants of this community were pioneers in just about every sense—they accepted the risk of coming to a place that had few amenities and was difficult to access, and literally cleared the way for the making of what the city was to become. And they willingly (many of them) accepted the challenge because they shared the same kind of optimism that Whitman discovered in examining the simultaneous opening of new territory and the building up of cities. It is fitting that this pioneering moment introduced the man who would so broaden the city's early industrial efforts that he would completely remake cultural and economic Lansing at the turn of the 20th century.

This book is an exploration of Lansing industry at the time immediately preceding the coming of the automobile and the reasons for its coming, the local career of the person most responsible for the modernization of the community, R.E. Olds, the industry that immediately grew out of the automobile trade, and R.E. Olds' life outside of automobiles and within the community. In order to focus best on these aspects of Lansing's industrial history and therefore see best the reasons for the early growth of the city (and Olds' place within it), the timeline here is inclusive of the period just after the dedication of the current Capitol building, in 1879, to the end of the automotive career of R.E. Olds, in 1936.

It should be noted that this is not a history of either Oldsmobile or of R.E. Olds' second automotive venture, REO. There has been much good scholarly and general interest literature on Oldsmobile's history. See, especially, Helen Early and Jim Walkinshaw's *Setting the Pace*. Also, since this study ends with Olds' departure from REO in 1936, no attempt has been made here to chronicle the entire corporate and social history of that company, which ended approximately 40 years after his departure.

Finally, it should be noted that while compiling the research and images for this project, it was discovered that any history of the industry of Lansing is by its nature a social history of its river, the Grand. Even before the city had a name, the earliest settlers and those who platted, mapped, and then established homesteads in Lansing all understood the crucial importance of this waterway. The city's industrial history simply would not exist without it. As is the case with Detroit, a damning gaze is often cast on this industrial history and on the early settlers and city planners as those who would not (and could not) foresee the damage inflicted in the first 100 years of manufacturing on the river's banks. But abuses to the Grand River have begun to be corrected. Industry has moved toward other venues within the expanded boundaries of the city, and with the building of the River Walk and parklands on its banks, Lansing began to embrace and celebrate the Grand in the last part of the 20th century.

One

INDUSTRIAL LANSING

BEFORE THE AUTOMOBILE

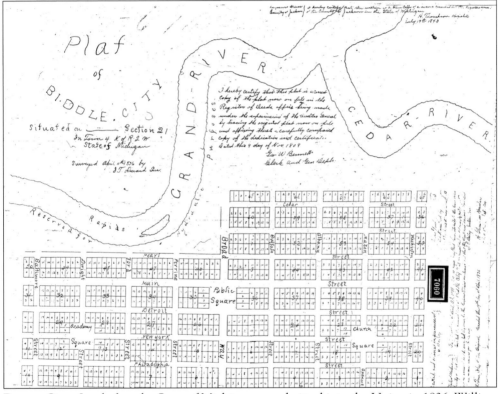

BIDDLE CITY. Just before the State of Michigan was admitted into the Union in 1836, William and Jerry Ford plotted land in mid-Michigan and were promoting it to Easterners from Lansing, New York. They called their town "Biddle City," located in what is now section 21, at the confluence of the Grand and Cedar Rivers. Few people that bought lots ever made it to see their swampy, heavily timbered properties, and some that did took one look and either went back East or settled in more hospitable territory. There were early settlers, though (Cooley, Townsend, and Seymore), that battled the elements and eventually made a go of it in lands purchased around Biddle City and elsewhere in nearby sections, and all settled around the Grand. This earliest plat of what is now Lansing also highlights the area that would become home to the city's most important industry, the manufacturing of automobiles.

TOWN OF MICHIGAN MAP. The state's constitution of 1835 declared Detroit as its temporary Capital, but required that the Capital be "permanently" located by the legislature by the year 1847. After the War of 1812, especially, it was thought by some that Detroit was too vulnerable because of its proximity to a foreign border. Many geographically central locations were entertained, including Ann Arbor and Jackson, because of their position on the main rails that led from Detroit to Chicago, but places such as Houghton and other northern locations were entertained as well, because of their importance in raw materials and trade. The wilderness that was Lansing at the time was thought a joke by many legislators, but it won the vote after a very confused and acrimonious debate led by Representative Enos Goodrich, of Genesee County. At the time the area of the city was known as "Michigan." (FPML/CADL.)

NEW CAPITOL. There were two Capitol buildings before this one, the Palladium-domed structure that we currently know as the state's seat of government. There was the structure in Detroit that was afterward used as a high school, and the "temporary" structure that was to eventually burn down in Lansing after the dedication of this building in 1879. The wide streets of Michigan Avenue in this photo (c. 1880) are yet unpaved, though what is now Grand River Avenue brought everyone previously invested in state politics to the new frontier capital on roads made of wooden planks, completed in 1853. (FPML/CADL.)

WASHINGTON AVENUE. This is a *c.* 1875 photo of early Washington Avenue. Horse-drawn wagons line the dirt road of the business center of the city at the time. Washington was the first road in Lansing to be paved, in 1878, with cedar planks down the middle and bordered by cobblestones. City planners soon found out that this was a bad method of paving, since the cedar would buckle and wear poorly with the extreme changes in Michigan weather. The same was found to be true with the Lansing-Howell Plank Road (now Grand River Avenue)—the main thoroughfare from Detroit to the new Capital—and the planks were replaced with gravel. It wasn't until 1893 that the first brick was laid on Lansing streets. (FPML/CADL.)

GRAND RIVER. From the Michigan Avenue Bridge, looking south, clapboard homes and small factories cling to the banks of the Grand River. In addition to the necessary construction of amenities for the incoming government workers, the industry of Lansing owes much of its beginnings to the rich supply of old-growth timber, its access to transport, and the hydraulic power that could be harnessed from the river. Though early pioneers used the river for travel between Jackson and Grand Rapids, its shallowness and the necessity of frequent portaging made for difficult going in larger vessels. (Henry B. Baker.)

North Lansing Depot. Rail was the other, if not preferred, method of transportation to and from Lansing in the city's early days. The Amboy, Lansing and Traverse Bay line (called the "Ram's Horn") was the first to connect Lansing to Detroit by direct rail, in 1861; and by 1863 it connected to the Lake Shore and Michigan Southern. Other lines were forthcoming—a route from Battle Creek in 1865, from Jackson in 1867, and the Grand Trunk opened service to Port Huron (and points east) in 1877. Commerce to and from the city were now secured and a free flow of goods could be established. Pictured is the Michigan Central station in North Lansing, with central and Pere Marquette traffic, c. 1900. At left is the passenger station, and looking northward is Lansing Spoke. (FPML/CADL.)

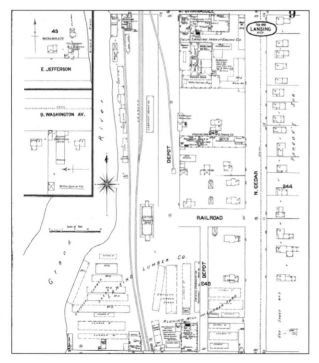

Depot, Sanborn. This Sanborn map from 1892 shows the main passenger and freight depot of the city, just north of Michigan Avenue and just east of the Grand River. Surrounding the depot and freight yards at the time were the Lansing Iron and Engine Co. (top) and Lansing Lumber (bottom), along Michigan. The actual passenger depot sits at the end of "Railroad" Street (later renamed Condit), just south of the freight yard that extends up toward Shiawassee. Though the depot operated for many years, it was prone to flood and subsequently impassable for the Michigan Central and Pere Marquette trains. It was later relocated to where Clara's restaurant now sits on Michigan Avenue.

INDUSTRIAL SCHOOL. Opened in 1856 as "House of Corrections for Young Offenders," and later given the more enlightened names "Michigan Reform School" and "Industrial School for Boys," the 30-acre facility stood on the grounds just north of what is now Eastern High School until the 1970s. It served as an alternative to the harsh realities of prison for young wrongdoers, though reports from the early days suggest it wasn't much different. Pictured is the Administration Building. (FPML/CADL.)

INDUSTRIAL SCHOOL, SANBORN. This Sanborn map from 1906 shows the extent of the Industrial School grounds. Its facilities included six "cottages" for residence, a chapel, play grounds, an "industrial building" where the boys would learn vocational training, and a hospital (not far from what is now the sprawling Sparrow Hospital complex). Though parents were allowed visitation, it is said that many of the incarcerated never heard from their families again after entering its grounds, where the boys would go to school in addition to learning a trade that they could apply in one of Lansing's many new factories when they were freed. Also featured here is another long-running state-sponsored institution—the Michigan School for the Blind.

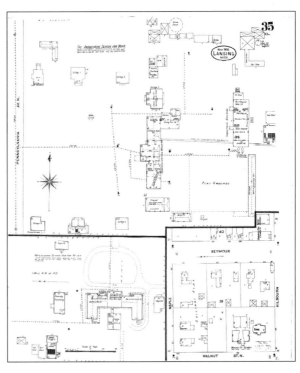

STEVENS & TAYLOR. This very early industrial photograph shows Stevens & Taylor Artificial Stone Works. Located on Michigan Avenue just east of the bridge and near the Michigan Central train depot, this spot would be the site of artificial stone works companies of some variety, and for some time. The sign on horse drawn cart says "Upper River Ice." In days before refrigeration, ice was "harvested" from lakes and rivers, and stored in warehouse-sized coolers. Given the amount of industry on the lower river and around the city's center, the name of this ice company is not surprising. Smaller companies such as these met the needs of a growing city, but the arrival of the 1870s would see industry in Lansing produce goods on a much larger scale. (FPML/CADL.)

BEMENT FACTORY. The building up of the Capital City after the Civil War coincided with the opening of the American West. The area's ample supply of lumber and the ease by which iron could be transported from the northern part of the state facilitated the manufacture of plows and agricultural tools that were in great demand. E. Bement & Sons (founded in 1869) would, by the 1880s, become one of the nation's leading suppliers of these tools and the city's largest manufacturing company. (Caterino/CADL.)

14

BEMENT WAGON. Also a great manufacturer of iron stoves and bobsleds, Bement was at the heart of the agricultural implement industry before the turn of the 20th century. Using an entire city block (south from Ionia, between Grand Avenue and the Grand River), the company's workforce swelled to over 400 at a time when few other manufacturers of the city employed 100. The banners of the wagon proclaim the growing success of the Lansing's leading manufacturer: Sales growth from $5k to $500k between 1870 and 1892; paid-in wages from $1,816k to $194,175k; and employees from 5 to 450. The banners also boast that Bement's products are sold all over the world. The company downsized locations during a depression in 1907, and its original location later housed the first facility for REO Truck. (FPML/CADL.)

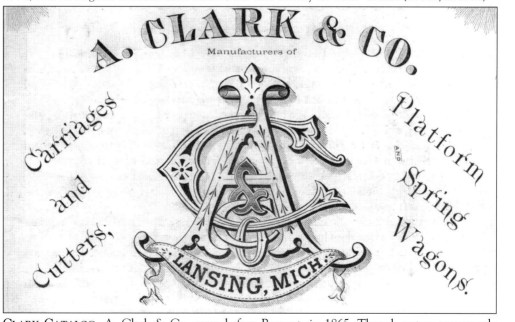

CLARK CATALOG. A. Clark & Co. came before Bement, in 1865. Though not as enormously profitable or renown, pioneer Albert Clark would develop this company out of a farrier shop to be one of the city's largest manufactures of fine carriages. Albert later trained his son, Frank, in the trade. Frank would for a time mirror the career of R.E. Olds. Pictured is the cover of the 1881 Clark catalog. (FPML/CADL.)

CLARK FACTORY. The three-story Clark factory was at the corner of Grand and Washtenaw. It was 150 by 125 feet and shared the banks of the Grand River with so many of the early factories who took advantage of the harvest of lumber floated up or downstream to be milled. Notice, as with most other factories of the time, the number of windows that would take best advantage of natural light in the days before a centralized lighting source, and compare to today's architecture of corrugated metal-boxed factories that rely exclusively on electric light. (Henry B. Baker.)

FRANK AND ALBERT CLARK. Pictured are Albert and Frank Clark in front of a carriage, demonstrating their wares. Nearing the end of a long career, Albert Clark's company was finally incorporated in 1897 during an economic depression, and with a capital of $50,000. At that time, Clark & Co. was competing with a number of other carriage manufacturers, including Powers Bros., Lansing Wagon Works, and Michigan Wheel (later Prudden, then Auto Wheel). Perhaps most important of all products made by the Clarks, though, was the body Frank Clark manufactured for the first of Olds' gasoline-powered vehicles. Also among the first investors in the Olds Motor Vehicle Co., in 1897, Frank later went on to start his own automotive and truck companies. (FPML/CADL.)

J.C. Schneider & Co. J.C. Schneider opened his own carriage and wagon shop at 112–114 E. Shiawassee after working for many years at Lansing Wagon Works. In this photo the firm displays its custom wagons, manufactured for local delivery companies—olden day tanker trucks. That Schneider opened his shop in the late 1890s and continued to manufacture these wagons into the second decade of the automobile demonstrates how slowly the public warmed to the new industry. By 1920, however, Schneider had retooled his shop to also build auto-truck bodies. (FPML/CADL.)

Lansing Wagon Works. First organized in 1881 (incorporated in 1887) at Grand and Shiawassee for the manufacture of farm wagons, Lansing Wagon Works grew to be the city's largest producer of carriages—turning out more than 5,000 per year by the late 1890s. The company's management included Fred Thoman (President), Merritt L. Coleman (Secretary), and E.F. Cooley (Treasurer). Cooley's name surfaces often in the course of the city's manufacturing history. By the late 1890s, he had become an industry giant in Lansing by helping to form the Michigan Supply Co., Maud S. Windmill & Pump, the Michigan Power Co., and especially serving as Vice President for both Olds Gasoline and Engine Co. and Olds Motor Vehicle Co. (FPML/CADL.)

LANSING WHEELBARROW CO. Lansing Wheelbarrow (later Lansing Co., incorporated in 1891), at the southwest corner of Cedar and Saginaw, was another important participant in the manufacturing history of the city—both for its product and its management. Its President was a man whose name is still well known to Lansing residents, E.W. Sparrow, and lesser known but equally important were the Secretary and Treasurer and Vice President, the Stebbins brothers, Arthur C. and Courtland Bliss. Notice the company's facilities bordering two train lines, for ease of shipping and receiving. (Caterino/CADL.)

LANSING WHEELBARROW. Pictured is a product from the Lansing Wheelbarrow's catalog, around the turn of the century. At this time the company was of the nation's largest suppliers of steel and wood wheelbarrows, hand trucks, and carts—producing over 80,000 units per year. Management would prove important in the automobile trade in Lansing in 1897, as E.W. Sparrow and A.C. Stebbins joined forces with R.E. Olds to develop mass production of the horseless carriage. Sparrow's initial investment secured him the position of President of Olds Motor Vehicle Co., the predecessor of what became Oldsmobile. (FPML/CADL.)

18

WHEELBARROW ASSEMBLY. Mass production before the 20th century, this photo shows part of the assembly line of Lansing Wheelbarrow. Before the days of the moving assembly line, factory workers often worked on sawhorses, drilling and hammering together parts that were delivered to them after being milled and shaped in a different part of the factory, or another factory altogether. In this image, workers assemble handcarts of the kind used to transport stacks of brick. The name change of Lansing Wheelbarrow to, simply, Lansing Co. not only reflected a diversified line of products, but also signaled the company's change of focus from supplying agricultural hardware to products of industrial and factory use. (FPML/CADL.)

LANSING SPOKE. The wheelwrights pictured on page 17 could have just as easily worked at Lansing Spoke Co. This ad (c. 1892) shows a quaint operation beside the place where the Michigan Central and Pere Marquette railroad tracks split—what were then the northern reaches of the city. As much a dealer in lumber as in carriage parts, this facility burned in 1894 and was quickly rebuilt further north, at 1508 Larch. As with many carriage suppliers of the time, the company was dissolved by the advent of the automobile, in this case taken over by Auto Wheel (the forerunner to Motor Wheel). (FPML/CADL.)

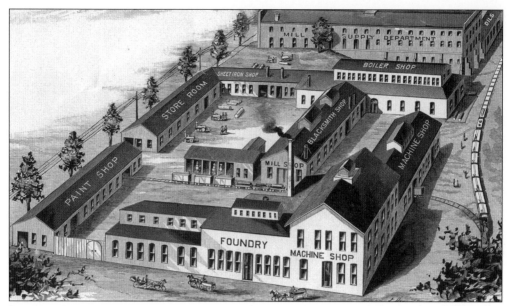

LANSING IRON AND ENGINE WORKS. Started as Lansing Iron Works, when incorporated in 1885 the name was changed to Lansing Iron and Engine works—reflecting a change in the city's manufacturing focus as makers of the stationary engine. One of the city's oldest big-money shops (its capital at the time of incorporation was the then-enormous sum of $250,000), it predates the opening of the new Capitol building. Located in the heart of what was then the major industrial corridor, at Shiawassee and Cedar, the factory shared the same block with Maud S. Windmill around the turn of the century. Notice the spur from the MCRR that runs straight into the heart of the complex. (FPML/CADL.)

LIEW. The stylized romanticism of the company's catalog view of itself is realized in this photo image, taken *c.* 1888. Orlando M. Barnes, former Mayor and President of LIEW, knew the value and importance of having multiple rail lines pass through the city because he also served as attorney and land commissioner for the Jackson, Lansing, and Saginaw Railroad Company from 1872 until his death in 1899. Railroad companies were given enormous amounts of land for the expense and responsibility of laying tracks, and the companies could also decide where, exactly, the tracks were to be laid. Entire towns went boom or bust during this kind of deal making. (Henry B. Baker.)

HUGH LYONS & CO. Hugh Lyons was Mayor during the earliest days of automobile manufacturing in Lansing. Also one of the city's early industry giants, his factory was on the less populated south branch of the river. At one time considered "the world's largest makers of store fixtures, show cases and wax figures," in latter days this was also an E.F. Cooley (Vice President) shop that was retooled to build parts for the automotive trade. (REOTM.)

PRUDDEN. Incorporated after the rise of the automobile, this plant at 701 May moved to the 700 block of East Saginaw and went on to become one of the titans of local industry. It was started as Michigan Wheel, then W.K. Prudden Co., and is today commonly referred to as Motor Wheel. Eventually conglomerating Lansing Spoke and Auto Body, Prudden was among the city's premier businesses at the turn of the century, and because of its adaptability was one of the most successful after the coming of the automobile. The company began as a manufacturer of wooden-spoked wheels, and by the time it was called Motor Wheel, produced a line of automobile and truck wheels, hubs and flanges, brake drums and disks, rims, and "stampings of all kinds," and boasted "largest exclusive manufactures of wheels for motor driven vehicles in the world." (Caterino/CADL.)

THOMAN MILLING CO. The Thoman Bros. occupied this spot for years in what is now called "Old Town," in the north part of the city and along the banks of the Grand. The area around Franklin Avenue (what is now called Grand River Avenue) was one of the first settled parts of Lansing and was considered the second "downtown" because of its train station, its concentration of shops on Turner Street, and the bustle of the workers coming and going from its many flour, grist, and saw mills. The Thomans were all industrious men—with interests in many local manufacturing concerns—but none were as important to the coming change in the city's industry as Fred, who at the turn of the century was also President of Lansing Wagon Works, and Vice President of Lansing Wheelbarrow. Notice the tracks running beside the mill—a spur from the MC line that would also feed another Lansing manufacturer at the turn of the century, Hildreth Motor & Pump. (REOTM.)

HILDRETH. Incorporated in 1901 as Hildreth Co., and lying on the east side of the Grand River just below the shops on Franklin and just north of the Thoman mill, this company went through many management changes. Eventually calling itself Hildreth Mfg. Co., the factory turned out what became the customary product for Lansing industry around the turn of the century—stationary gas engines and castings. Perhaps most important in its managerial history is that Richard H. Scott was eventually the company's President after it became known as Novo Engine. Scott would partner with R.E. Olds in the creation of REO, and for a time serve as President of that company, from 1915 to the early 1930s. (FPML/CADL.)

CIGAR MAKERS UNION. By the late 1890s there were at least ten cigar manufacturers in Lansing, which put the city's output on a national scale. Though unions existed and they all met at the Central Labor Hall, there was little unionization of the bulk of the city's industrial workforce around this time. Cigar makers were among the few who organized, and the banner carried in this parade represents Local 272 of the Cigar Makers International Union of America. At the center of the local cigar trade was the flamboyant James Hammell, who brought the Hammell Cigar Co. to Lansing in August of 1893. Hammell also served as Mayor from 1900 to 1903 during the campaign that brought R.E. Olds and Oldsmobile back to Lansing, from its brief stay in Detroit, through a creative land deal engineered by the Lansing Business Men's Association. FPML/CADL.)

LANSING BREWERY. Other kinds of manufacturing shared the industrial corridor with the mills and motor manufacturers. Early on there were two large breweries between Saginaw and Franklin, and then came the Lansing Brewing Co., incorporated March 16, 1898, and located at 1301–1309 Turner. Though a 1906 ad for the LBC proclaimed that its beer was "Bottled Expressly for Family Use," the often temperance-preaching management of factories battled to keep the workforce sober even when workers were away from the job. Also of note is the brewery's President and General Manager, Lawrence Price, who was an original investor in REO. (FPML/CADL.)

LANSING SUGAR CO. Yet another kind of industrial giant emerged in the city around the turn of the 20th century—the Lansing Sugar Co. (also known as Owasso Sugar Co.) Incorporated in 1902 with a capital of $1.25 million, the company converted sugar beets into sugar on a grand scale. Located at 501 North, the factory was at the far reaches of the city, beside what is now the north part of Grand River Avenue. Such a large operation could not only supply the city's workers with a large amount of jobs and income, but would also greatly benefit the area's many farmers. (FPML/CADL.)

TRANSPORTATION, c. 1898. During a patriotic celebration on the 100 block of South Washington, we can see the many modes of transportation that were in use just before the automobile. Notice the variety of horse-drawn wagons and the presence of what was thought to be a fad at the time—the bicycle. The streets are paved with brick in this downtown center, and the tracks of the Washington Street trolley are visible at bottom. Businesses of note are the Lansing State Savings Bank (J. Edward Roe, Cashier) and the long-standing shop of J.W. Edmonds & Sons (father of J.P. Edmonds). Also at center is the Lansing YWCA, at 121 South Washington. (FPML/CADL.)

FIRE DEPARTMENT. Lansing quickly outgrew its first form of fire control—a volunteer bucket brigade—and in 1857 chartered its first fire department. Pictured is Fire Department Station No. 1, located on the 100 block of North East, c. 1903. On the eve of the city's transportation and industrial transformation, the streets are bricked for greater ease of travel. Featured in this photograph are (from left to right) a hook and ladder unit, a chemical unit, and a hose unit. The chief's carriage fronts the image. Notice the agricultural business at left, Bidwell Threshers, with its open double-wide doors where a farm wagon could back right into the store to be loaded with merchandise. (Caterino/CADL.)

CAPITAL, c. 1895. Michigan Avenue has its first iron bridge in this view, taken from the Water Works "standpipe" c. 1895. Previous wooden bridges were, like planked roads, found to wear poorly and require constant maintenance. The lack of commerce in the foreground, at the river's eastern edge, is due to the enormous amount of property occupied by the rail companies for freight storage and service. Also notable is the Michigan Supply Co., at far right and just above the river at Grand and Ottawa. The company was E.F. Cooley's, who came to the city to start a gas-fixture supply wholesale, would become instrumental in beginning Olds' automobile concerns, and by the early 20th century seemed to be involved with just about all manufacturing in Lansing. (FPML/CADL.)

SANBORN MAP, 1885. The city was growing into its industrial potential in this Sanborn map, from 1885. Mostly hemmed in by Franklin (now Grand River) to the north, Lenawee to the south, Logan (now MLK, not pictured) to the west, and the train tracks of the MC and PM railroads to the east. The black demarcations along the Grand all represent factories. Along the west side of the river, from bottom, is Lansing Wheel Works, Clark & Co., E. Bement (just in front of the gas works), Buck's Furniture, Lansing Wagon Works, then two of the city's breweries between Franklin and Saginaw. On the east side from bottom to top are Capital City Mfg., Stevens Artificial Stone (also Oriental Mills), Lansing Iron & Engine Works, Lansing Wheelbarrow, then Schofields Mill, Hart's Flour Mill, Capital Flour, and finally the North Lansing Planning Mill just north of Franklin. Still a fledgling, one-room building at this time and not shown on the map is the shop of P.F. Olds & Son, just south of Clark & Co., along the west bank of the Grand—a shop that would change the city, and the world, within the next 15 years.

26

Two
From River Street to
Olds Motor Works

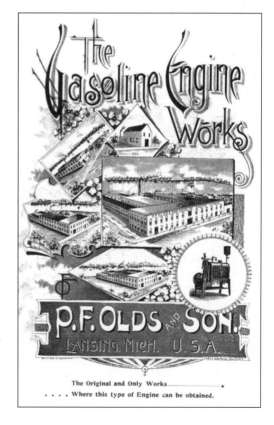

P.F. Olds & Son Catalog. This cover
from a late 19th century catalog for P.F.
Olds & Son demonstrates the growth of
the company from the time Pliny brought
his family to Lansing and opened shop in
the early 1880s, to the days just before his
son's emergence as the first automobile
mass manufacturer. The centerpiece
factory illustration is bordered by images of
the growth of the pioneer shop on River
Street and the product that gave it
national recognition—the stationary
engine. (REOTM.)

MICHIGAN AVENUE, c. 1898. Compare this view of Michigan Avenue at Grand with the one on page 10 and notice the differences to the city's streets. Electric arc lighting, telephone wires, and rail cars share the now cobbled streets with the old horse and buggy. This is a view of a town in the midst of great change, and at the brink of the modern world. (FPML/CADL.)

SOUTH WASHINGTON, c. 1898. Lansing's first electric arc light was installed in 1885. Its first public transportation (horse-drawn trolleys) began in 1886, and its first electric trolley lines arrived in 1890. In 1904, the city's electric rail lines first connected to the interurban lines of neighboring communities. But nothing could compare to the ease of travel that the automobile would bring, and all public transportation in Lansing (except of course busses) was eventually cut off by the arrival of the gasoline engine. (FPML/CADL.)

OLDS AT BIRTHPLACE, GENEVA, OHIO. Pliny F. Olds and his wife, Sarah, were parents to four boys and one girl—Ransom Eli being the youngest child. Pliny was a blacksmith, machinist, farmer, and ironworker who moved his family around north central Ohio in search of work that was profitable and that suited him. Pictured is the house in Geneva where young R.E. (as he preferred to be called) spent his earliest years. At left in the photo is the blacksmith shop where Pliny sometimes worked as a farrier and where the boy Olds began his lifelong dislike of horses—something that would be cultivated when he was made curator of the family stable after they moved to Lansing. (Gladys Olds Anderson.)

R.E. OLDS AT 16. R.E. Olds was 16 years old when his father traded the farm in Ohio for a house and two lots on River Street and moved the family to Lansing in 1880. Even in 1880, with a population of approximately 8,000, the new Michigan city would have seemed like a metropolis to the young farm boy. Young Olds took almost immediately to working in the family business along with his older brother, Wallace, who was a partner to his father. By 1885, at age 21, R.E. Olds had bought out his brother's interest in the motor manufacture and repair shop. (OHC.)

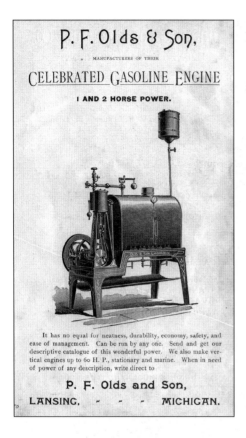

P.F. OLDS & SON AD. By 1886 Olds was hard at work with his advancements in stationary engines. His great invention at the time was a gasoline motor that much more quickly heated a steam engine for work, such as in printing presses, which needed to be stopped and started frequently. Pictured is the kind of small, relatively portable model that could have a belt attached to the wheel at lower left, for use of turning machines like drills, saws, and pumps. By the late 1880s, the motors of P.F. Olds & Son were nationally recognized, and the city of Lansing was on its way to becoming a motor capital. (REOTM.)

EXPANDED OLDS SHOP. Pictured is the second incarnation of P.F. Olds & Son on River Street, the Gas Engine Works. R.E. is standing next to bearded Pliny, at right. The first shop (18 by 24 feet) was practically a shed compared to this 50 by 100 foot 1896 expansion. Olds went to business school for a short time, but spent most of his spare hours tinkering with his "experimental" horseless carriages here in his spare hours. The success and building up of his father's motor business was finally what provided capital enough to start Olds Motor Works. (MSUAHC.)

STEAMERS ON THE GRAND. The ad copy on page 30 lists "vertical engines up to 60 H.P., stationary and marine" as the product line for P.F. Olds & Son. Pictured are pleasure boaters out for a steam-powered ride on the Grand River, at what is now Waverly Park. It is often overlooked that Olds spent many formative years on the Grand—a rather shallow river good for hydroelectric power, but also for shallow-hulled boating. Especially down river, toward what is now Waverly Avenue and above the dam just west of the "Big Bend," Olds could often test his boat motors. This early industrial interest became a lifetime passion. (FPML/CADL.)

OLDS' FIRST STEAM HORSELESS. Around the time Olds was "finishing" his first self-propelled horseless carriage, the business he built with his father was expanding further—capital stock reaching $12,000 in 1887. Other steam vehicles of locomotion had been built before Olds tried his hand, so this wasn't especially novel for its time. But this one was engineered by Olds, and after a noisy early-morning ride that terrified Lansing residents in its first and only run, the inventor tore it down to see how he could build it better. Even his father, who was watching the River Street shop grow, doubted his son. (OHC.)

SCIENTIFIC AMERICAN PHOTO, 1892. *Scientific American* was the celebration of all things industrial in the late 19th century. Because of Olds' success with steam and gas motors, the magazine was aware of the Olds shop and covered his latest invention with praise. Olds took the opportunity to assail the advantages of going horseless, saying that his machine "never kicks or bites, never tires out on long runs . . . does not require care in the stable, and only eats when on the road." This is the second of Olds' steam-powered horseless carriages. After the publicity, Olds was contacted by the Francis Times Co. of London, who purchased the vehicle for their Bombay, India branch. Stories vary on the fate of this vehicle; some suggesting it sank with its transporting ship on route to India (" . . . And the company was saved . . . " remarked Olds), while some say it served the Francis Company well for many years. (OHC.)

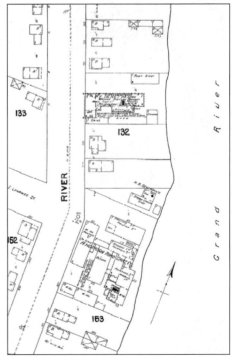

P.F. OLDS, SANBORN, 1892. The 1890s treated the Olds shop well, especially due to the ingenuity and business savvy of Ransom. In 1893 the capital stock increased to $30,000. Pictured is a Sanborn map of the Olds shop just before it became a Lansing giant, expanding further its capital stock as well as its real estate around the River Street grounds. The grounds of the Anderson Road Cart Co. (just below the Olds shop) would be taken over by Olds' expansion. One of Anderson's principal investors was the wealthy local resident, E.W. Sparrow, whose financial backing Olds would seek in order to develop, build, and mass-produce horseless carriages.

THIRD HORSELESS CARRIAGE. In 1896 Olds rode the streets of Lansing with his third horseless carriage (pictured), and what was also his first gasoline-powered model. Almost simultaneously in Michigan did Olds, Henry Ford, and Charles King demonstrate a "first" in gas-powered automobiles, though Olds was the first to start a company for the sole purpose of producing them. Pictured are Olds (at tiller) and Frank Clark, who was Olds' industrial neighbor (at Clark & Co.) and the builder of the body of this early automobile. In the back seat are their wives, Metta Olds and Harriet Clark. (OHC.)

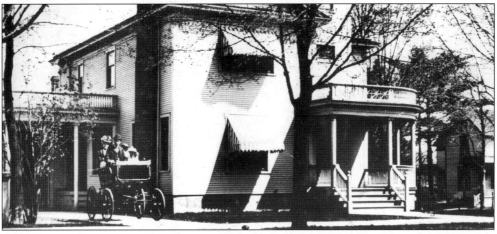

OLDS HOME, GRAND AND KALAMAZOO. With the success of P.F. Olds & Son, the Olds family moved into this house, not far from the River Street shop, at Grand and Kalamazoo. The house is said to have the city's first built-on carport. It was about this time that Olds began looking for investors to expand his industrial interests toward making horseless carriages. The obvious place to look for financial backing in automobile making was Chicago, where expositions of the horseless were celebrated regularly, and there was already some manufacturing happening, though it was mostly in electric models. In Edward Sparrow, Olds found an enthusiastic and wealthy businessman, who was also President of the local City National Bank (E.F. Cooley was Vice President). Together with Arthur C. Stebbins, Frank Clark, Samuel L Smith, and a few others they formed the Olds Motor Vehicle Works. (Gladys Olds Anderson.)

"PERFECT." At the first Board of Directors' meeting it was decided in this now-famous document that R.E. Olds would be elected Manager of the new company, and directed "that the Manager be authorized to build one perfect [then crossed out] carriage in as nearly perfect a manner as possible and complete it at the earliest possible moment." Olds' work, it seems, was cut out for him, and it would take him into the turn of the 20th century to get the manufacturing of his automobiles moving. What the company had going for it, though, was the success of the River Street shop (at this point Olds Gas Engine Works) and its continued source of revenue to cover losses incurred over the next four years of development. (OHC.)

OGEW STOCK. Though E.F. Cooley first received only one share of the new vehicle company, he received 2,200 shares of the Gas Engine Works (at this point operating as a separate concern) and was made Vice President. There were other prominent names, like James P. Edmonds, now invested in the company Olds' father started in 1880, but Olds was still Manager and President.

It later became clear, however, that those invested in the new vehicle company were much more interested in the already profitable gas engine factory, and R.E. Olds felt his control in the latter slipping. He had sold major interests in the Gas Engine Works in order to finance capital for building automobiles, and about this time (in 1898) he realized that this capital wasn't enough to get the auto company rolling. (Caterino/CADL.)

34

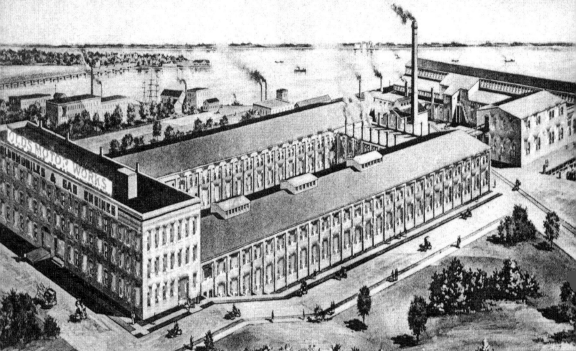

Hold Card to light.   Detroit Factory and Main Offices of Olds Motor Works

DETROIT FACTORY, OLDS MOTOR WORKS. This was the first factory for the sole purpose of producing automobiles. In the first year of production, the Olds Motor Vehicle Co. made a mere four vehicles in the shops of the River Street factory. Production of gas engines, however, continued to climb. Olds knew he needed to get out of the River Street shop and into a separate factory if he were to ever get the automobile company into production, but even with previous sales of stock and re-incorporations he felt he still lacked the finances. Then again, in 1898, the company was reinvested with the even greater stock of $50,000. With the new investments Olds retained the majority of ownership, but Cooley, F. Thoman, and Rueben Shettler got a greater share than before, as did M.F. Bates, Richard Scott, Pliny Olds, R.E. Handy, and most importantly, S.L. Smith's son, Frederick—the only Detroiter of the group. But the capital was still not enough and in 1899, upon returning from a trip to the East Coast where Olds entertained many offers to move the company, he all but sold the engine shop to Samuel L. Smith for the capitalization of $500,000 in the now-renamed Olds Motor Works. Olds had given up controlling interest in the family business, and it was moving from his hometown of Lansing to Detroit (although the River Street shop would keep running). Pictured is the five-acre parcel of the Detroit plant of the Olds Motor Works, situated between Jefferson Avenue and the Detroit River, next to the Belle Isle Bridge. (Caterino/CADL.)

OLDS TRAP. Though other cities were considered for the move at the time (including Cleveland, Toledo, Indianapolis, and Buffalo), Detroit was the obvious choice because of its burgeoning industrial market, and it is no wonder why it eventually became the Motor City. The city provided many industrial and cosmopolitan amenities that Lansing simply did not (including paved roads), and especially, provided easy access to Great Lakes shipping and rail service. Pictured are R.E. Olds and Roy Chapin in the front seat of this early model "Trap" at the Detroit facility. In these early stages, OMW was mainly in development and had many models. (OHC.)

ELECTRICS ON BELLE ISLE. Production was slow early on, partly because Olds and his engineers were not convinced of which mode of power was best for locomotion. Even the great developer of the gasoline motor thought electric was to be the fuel of the future, at the time. Here an early Olds publicity shot shows off the ease with which these the Olds electric models could be handled—by women dressed in their finest and the young. The shot is taken in front of the Belle Isle Police Station. Belle Isle was the first "proving grounds" for OMW. (OHC.)

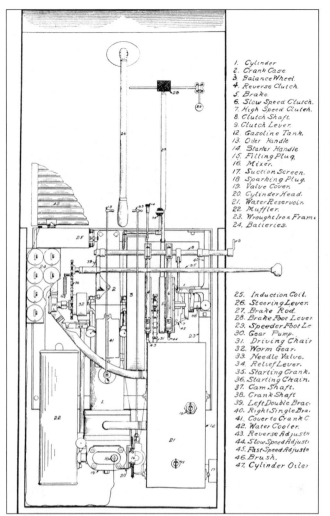

1. Cylinder
2. Crank Case
3. Balance Wheel
4. Reverse Clutch
5. Brake
6. Slow Speed Clutch
7. High Speed Clutch
8. Clutch Shaft
9. Clutch Lever
12. Gasoline Tank
13. Oiler Handle
14. Starter Handle
15. Filling Plug
16. Mixer
17. Suction Screen
18. Sparking Plug
19. Valve Cover
20. Cylinder Head
21. Water Reservoir
22. Muffler
23. Wrought Iron Frame
24. Batteries

25. Induction Coil
26. Steering Lever
27. Brake Rod
28. Brake Foot Lever
29. Speeder Foot Le
30. Gear Pump
31. Driving Chair
32. Worm Gear
33. Needle Valve
34. Relief Lever
35. Starting Crank
36. Starting Chain
37. Cam Shaft
38. Crank Shaft
39. Left Double Brac
40. Right Single Bra
41. Cover to Crank C
42. Water Cooler
43. Reverse Adjustm
44. Slow Speed Adjustm
45. Fast Speed Adjustm
46. Brush
47. Cylinder Oiler

OLDS CURVED DASH TRANSPARENCY, TOP VIEW. The early days of gasoline engine and automobile making were the times of true manufacturing pioneers. Though Olds regularly protected his work by filing and receiving patents for his inventions in the field (he held 20 before 1906), he wanted everyone to understand his advancements and forward the field of progress. Because he wanted everyone to have an automobile, and to therefore see his vision of the future realized, he rarely called infringements of these patents. And then along came George B. Selden, who threatened the free flow of information between auto makers by filing for royalties he thought due to him because of a patent he filed in 1896 for the gasoline automobile engine he had invented (but never tested). Some of the companies who were beginning to manufacture autos at the time formed an alliance that could be bought into and which then protected them from the suit. This infuriated Olds, especially because he thought the suit would mean a monopoly on invention within the industry, and because he thought the claim was bogus. The Smiths, however, outvoted Olds and joined the Association of Licensed Automobile Manufacturers. It was the first great wedge between Olds and the Smiths, and the beginning of the end with his association with the company. Pictured is a diagram of the Olds Curved Dash model. One of the reasons for Oldsmobile's early success was that it used a catalog of parts that were photographed and not drawn, which could be used for comparison and understanding the new technology. (OHC.)

A Tale of Two Streets. Olds' vision for the future also included the necessary paving of streets in order for the automobile to run more efficiently. This ad shows a downtown center with and without the new method of transportation. The people on the right enjoy the "clean city" as they shop in their finest, stroll upon concrete sidewalks, and drive in their Oldsmobiles. The frontier-like town at left is stuck in the "horse age," which apparently means without people or economy (note the "For Sale" sign above the business). Also to note is the often-used slogan, "Nothing to Watch but the Road," another way of demonizing the temperamental nature of what Olds thought was an outmoded means of transportation—the horse. (OHC.)

Chapin Ad. Although the address of OMW in these advertisements says Detroit, Mich., they date from a time when the factory had burned almost completely in March of 1901 and then moved back to Lansing. The only model saved from the fire was the (pictured) Curved Dash "Runabout," which was pushed out of the burning factory by timekeeper James J. Brady. Because all models, blueprints, and patterns of other cars were destroyed, the Curved Dash became the sole production model of OMW. The "Runabout" then revolutionized the fledgling industry because of its lightweight construction, its durability, and its price of $650, which the masses could afford. (OHC.)

MAP OF LANSING, c. 1900. After the wresting of the seat of state government from the city of Detroit, it might be said that the fire at OMW in Detroit in 1901 was the single most important thing to happen to Lansing. The Lansing Business Men's Association (forerunner to the Chamber of Commerce) was quick to pitch a deal to the troubled company that would bring the great promise of jobs and economy back to the Lansing area. The job of the LBMA was to recruit business concerns to the area at the turn of the century. Officers, which include familiar names within this book, were James J. Baird (President), A.A. Piatt (Vice President), J. Edward Roe (Treasurer), O.A. Jenison (Secretary), as well as J.B. Seager, Lawrence Price, C.E. Bement, and others. The group succeeded in doubling nearly every aspect of economy in the city between 1900 and the time just after the arrival of OMW: the capital invested increased by nearly 200 percent, salaries paid and number of workers by more that 100 percent, and the total value of products made increased by 134 percent—then at nearly $7,000,000. At the time the State Fair Grounds were situated on the Grand River, along the Grand Trunk rail lines in the very southwest end of the city (pictured lower right), and this would be the property offered to Olds, the Smiths, and the stockholders for coming back to Lansing. Notice the smokestacks of aforementioned factories along the Grand in the center of the map. (FPML/CADL.)

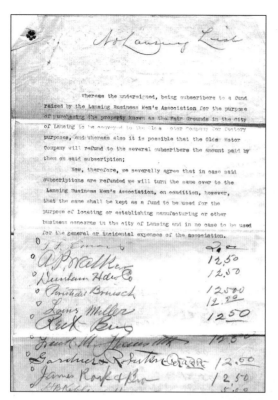

LBMA Subscription. In order to pay for the State Fair Grounds land given to OMW in the effort to lure the company back to Lansing ,an old-fashioned collection was taken up with area businessmen. It was a good-will gesture made to induce OMW into feeling wanted, and it worked. There are five pages of hand-written signatures to this document, each with the corresponding dollar amount pledged. Small shops paid as little as $5, while businessmen with larger interests (like E.F. Cooley) promised more than $100, knowing or at least hoping they would see their own businesses grow with the addition of such a large factory. (FPML/CADL.)

Lansing State Savings Ledger and Check. The total amount for the cost of the Fair Grounds land was $4,750. The ledger shows individual payments over time, from September of 1901 to December 28 of 1902, and in increments as low as $50 and as much as $815 in one of the first payments. As of the end of 1902, the note still carried a balance of $725. (FPML/CADL.)

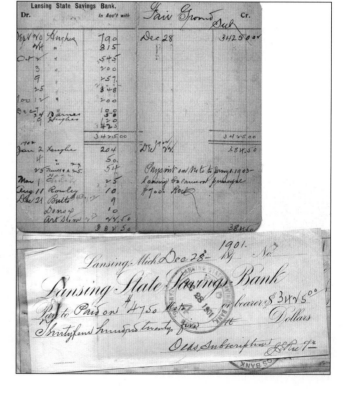

40

Lansing State Savings Bank.

CAPITAL PAID IN $150,000.

Nov. 14, 1902.

Lansing, Mich.

Mr. O. A. Jenison,

Secy Lansing Business Mens Assocn.,

Dear Sir:---- I write to call your attention to the note of $4750.00 less endorsements, made for the purchase of the Fair Ground property in the Olds Motor Co. matter, and while this paper is a very strong paper by reason of its numerous endorsements, from a Bankers standpoint it is in a very undesirable situation, being over a year past due. It strikes me that it is time that some steps were taken to retire it. By calling the attention of the proper parties to this, and taking some steps along the line suggested, you will oblige,

Very respectfully,

[signature]

LANSING STATE SAVINGS NOTE TO LBMA. J. Edward Roe, Cashier of the Lansing State Savings Bank, here writes to O.A. Jenison because of the "undesirable situation" of the past due bank note on the Fair Grounds in 1902. The letter is not exactly threatening in tone, though, because as Roe says, the paper is "strong . . . by reason of its numerous endorsements." By virtue of all the regular payments shown in the previous document, it is obvious that the LBMA hadn't forgotten about the outstanding note, but the amounts seem to have dwindled with every deposit. Interesting to note is Roe's future connection to R.E. Olds, as Roe's son, Clarence, later married Olds' daughter, Bernice. J. Edward Roe was also one of the original investors in the Bates Automobile Co., and eventually Secretary and Treasurer of REO. (FPML/CADL.)

OMW LANSING FACTORY. The LBMA could see its investment at work almost immediately. On the site of the State Fair Grounds, the second OMW factory was quickly built in order to get into production of the Curved Dash Olds and recoup losses from the Detroit fire and subsequent move back to Lansing. The city's stock of skilled labor also increased dramatically with the new facility, as did an influx of cargo on its shipping lines and the amount of money paid to other local business. (OHC.)

ROY CHAPIN, 1901. Though so many now know of the cross-country trek of Horatio Jackson, few know of the first long-distance journey of its kind, taken by Roy Chapin. One of the few people in this book born to have been born in Lansing, Chapin's father was a prominent lawyer in town and would have been known to people like the Olds, Sparrows, and Cooleys. While attending University of Michigan, Roy met Howard Coffin, who eventually lured Chapin to Detroit to work in the new Olds Motor Works—as a photographer of parts for the catalog (which would show that parts really existed), but also as a general worker and "tester" of the cars on Belle Isle. R.E. Olds was a tireless promoter of his product in the early days, driving the streets of Lansing whenever possible, and to fairs in Ionia and other neighboring communities to show ruggedness and drivability in all kinds of conditions. For the New York Auto Show of 1901, he equipped Roy Chapin with a Curved Dash model loaded with extra parts, and the trip began in Detroit on October 27. The journey was a struggle through rough terrain and bad weather, but there was only one major mechanical breakdown—when Chapin snapped a main spring while driving into a field to avoid an agitated farmer. Tires were a nuisance to keep inflated, the one-cylinder engine needed many replacements of gaskets, and there was constant maintenance of oil and water, but Chapin made it relatively unscathed to the Waldorf-Astoria on November 5. The publicity generated over 1,000 orders, and OMW was saved. Chapin went on to start his own car companies, including Hudson, and became an ambassador for the paving of American roads. (REOTM.)

OMW Lansing Postcard. After the New York Auto Show, orders for the Curved Dash came pouring in. Chapin's feat of averaging 14 miles per hour in the seven-and-a-half-day trip was a marvel to the skeptical and made a believer of many. Much of the public was swayed by the cost-effectiveness of automobile versus horse ownership, and the wealthy were just curious. In 1902 OMW built and shipped 2,000 units, and the standard for mass manufacturing of automobiles was set. Other figures for production during the management reign of R.E. Olds were: 3,924 in 1903, and 5,000 in 1904—the year that Olds left the company. This postcard shows the test track, to the west of the factory, left over from the Fair Grounds. (Caterino/CADL.)

Shop floor, OMW. Though taken during a slightly later time frame than other images in this chapter, this photo shows well what it would have been like to work on the machining floor of OMW in its early days. The photo is also a good demonstration of some of the many ways an early gas motor could be put to use. Motors were fitted with belts that would turn the machines on the shop floor. (OHC.)

MAXWELL AND OLDS, c. 1902. Pictured are R.E. Olds and Jonathan D. Maxwell demonstrating the power and durability of the Runabout. The early Olds vehicle companies were the places through which many of the pioneers of the automobile industry would get their start. Maxwell was also a gasoline engine maker before joining the ranks of OMW as a tester, then leaving in 1902 to eventually join with the Briscoe Brothers in making the Maxwell-Briscoe (eventually incorporated by Chrysler Corporation). The Briscoes were the first to make bodies (in mass quantities), Henry Leland (founder of Cadillac) was enlisted to build motors, and the Dodge Brothers made transmissions—all for the first Oldsmobiles. This is not to mention all of the people who worked in early Olds factories and went on to either start their own automobile and engine companies or rise to the highest ranks in Oldsmobile or REO. It is also worth noting that Henry Ford was a regular visitor to the early Olds facilities, in both Lansing and Detroit, to study production. From this lineage R.E. Olds would later get the nickname "Schoolmaster." (OHC.)

SMOOTH RIDE OF THE OLDSMOBILE. For years the early automobile industry would have to prove itself to the wary American public. Feats of all kinds were staged to show the automobile was worthy of switching to, and such feats were performed in all kinds of places where people gathered. Here a balancing act is performed while the Curved Dash ascends a steep grade to show the smoothness of the vehicle's ride, even in instances of great torque. (MSUAHC.)

RURAL PUBLICITY PHOTO, c. 1903. Oldsmobile was also a pioneer in advertising, the first to nationally do so in the *Saturday Evening Post*. Early advertisements emphasized strength in construction, ease in control, smoothness in ride, and above all economy. Horse owners were asked to compare the cost of keeping and feeding a horse for a year to the cost of owning an automobile that used just one gallon of gasoline every 40 miles. The hardest market to sell to was the rural population, who lived in territories where paved roads were non-existent. This photo was actually taken not far from the OMW factory in Lansing, where, at the time, one need not go far to be in the hinterland. (OHC.)

WHITMAN AND HAMMOND, 1903. During the same summer (1903) Dr. Horatio Nelson Jackson received credit for completing the now-famous first transcontinental trip across the United States in his Winton-made automobile, Lester Whitman and Eugene Hammond attempted to do the same, though in a much lighter Curved Dash Olds. Pictured here, the two receive a letter from San Francisco Mayor Schmitz for delivery to New York City Mayor Low. Through incredibly difficult terrain and many mechanical breakdowns, the two made it to the East Coast considerably behind the Winton and the second car to make the trip, a Packard—though it was a victory for Oldsmobile of unexpected proportions. Because of the car's small size and low price relative to the other two much heavier models, the Oldsmobile was heralded as "the most remarkable of the three," and which proved great advertisement for the automobile and for the company. These cross-country races also proved to advertise another of Olds' recurring campaigns for increased funding for roads, which he knew would open up the world for new possibilities in transportation and commerce. Whitman, incidentally, smashed Jackson's cross-country speed record the next year, in 1904, again set the record 1906, and in 1910 would break the record one more time with Eugene Hammond. (MSUAHC.)

ELKS CARNIVAL PARADE, 1903. Though automobile parades were becoming a regular part of the annual Auto Show in NYC, on the East Coast, this is an image of the first such event in Lansing. The photo shows the stretch of Washington Avenue between Michigan and Allegan. Both Oldsmobile and REO would continue this tradition in the early 20th century, for the purposes of galvanizing the community around its most important industrial product, but also for the purpose of marketing new models and product lines. (OHC.)

TRANSPORTATION IN THE CAPITAL CITY. This *c.* 1903 photo demonstrates the different kinds of transportation available to the people of Lansing, in a demonstration of civic pride. The trolley tracks on Michigan Avenue looped north on Capitol, but ran on Washington as well. Teamsters circle the Olds Runabout and its competitor, the horse. It wasn't until well into the 1910s that people of the city were convinced of the automobile, and horses all but disappear from photographs. (OHC.)

OLDS GASOLINE ENGINE WORKS. By 1903, R.E. Olds was at odds with the Smiths over many managerial decisions, and about the direction of the company. The Smiths, especially Frederick, wanted to move ahead and begin building heavier, more expensive models, as was becoming the norm in the U.S., and particularly in Europe. Olds insisted that the success of the company was in its inexpensive model for the masses and would remain so in the future. In the spring of 1904, at the height of popularity of the Curved Dash, Olds began selling of his shares of stock and left the company. When he quit the company, he also left behind the River Street shop forever. (OHC.)

ORIGINAL PLANT SITE. Upon Olds' exit, Frederick L. Smith assumed the position of General Manager at the Lansing factory, and the Detroit shop was closed. Oldsmobile then floundered in the next few years because of managerial indecisiveness, and by 1906 sales had actually fallen back to the levels of 1902. When William C. Durant started General Motors in the fall of 1908 Oldsmobile joined almost immediately, and the company was saved. The company that Ransom Eli Olds began as an outgrowth of his father's engine shop would expand in Lansing to include several plant sites and go on to be one of the greatest producers of automobiles in world history, eventually exceeding one million cars per year in the latter 20th century. Pictured is the original site given by the LBMA, expanded to this view from 1966. (OHC.)

Three
REO
OLDS RISES AGAIN

R.E. OLDS, c. 1905. When Olds left Olds Motor Works in 1903 because of a power struggle and arguments with the Smiths over the direction of the company, he boarded a train to California for a family vacation. There he met with Reuben Shettler, an ex-Lansing resident and investor in Olds' early automotive interests who had become an Oldsmobile dealer in Los Angeles. The two began a discussion about the possibility of a new company. Olds is pictured here around the time of his second foray into the business of manufacturing automobiles. (OHC.)

HUGH LYONS. After a long industrial career in Lansing, Hugh Lyons became Mayor of the city in 1904—the year the city would secure its second great automobile company. Lansing's industry and economy were booming, thanks in large measure to the enormous amount of materials and manpower that were employed in getting the Olds Motor Works factory up and running. Lyons was also an original investor in REO, along with a familiar cast of players to Lansing industry: Edward F. Peer, Lawrence Price, J. Edward Roe, William and Edgar Porter, Benjamin E. Davis, S. Elgin Mifflin, Charles P. Downey, and James J. Baird. (FPML/CADL.)

REO DEAL, JULY 4, 1904. Pictured is the one of the original "secret" drafts that describes how the company's stock was to be divided, with Olds getting the controlling interest for his patents, his "knowledge and good-will of the trade," and the guarantee that Olds will remain with the company for at least five years. The document also names E.F. Peer (who was once a Clerk for Shettler at Huber Co.) as Secretary and Treasurer partly because he is "an easy and modest man to get along with." Also of note is end of paragraph two, which considers property owned by Olds on Michigan Avenue as potential for the factory site. The document would have been a secret for many reasons, including Shettler's concurrent employment selling Oldsmobiles. (FPML/CADL.)

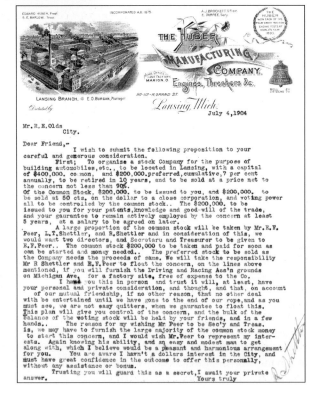

50

Olds Motor Works,   LANSING, MICH. Aug. 19, '04.

    Detroit, Mich.

Gentlemen:- Replying to your favor of the 18th. beg to say that, the

papers for the new Company were filed last Tuesday *the 16th* and the State has

authorized us to commence business under the name of "R.E.Olds Co.,

Our name does not in any way appear like the Olds Motor Work's. As far

as the name Olds is concerned, I think that if you were to refer to the

name of Smith, Jones or Brown, you would find that they would all have

to stay out of business as far as their name was concerned. The name

of our car certainly will not be a name that will in any way sound like

Olds Mobile. Personally I can say, that 30 days ago I never intended

to enter the automobile business again; I have only done so because the

trade in general requested me to do so; numerous friends of mine through

out the U.S. have urged this upon me, while the people in my own town

organized and had the stock all signed up before they submitted the prop-

osition to me. My ambition in the old Company, had I remained manager,

would have been to have done a business this year of not less than 3,500

000.00; I consider that it was a very easy matter when you take into con-

sideration the start the Company had. I regret very much to learn that,

for the first time since the Company was organized in 1890 that this

year it will do a decreasing business, as I am told that the sales will

be about half what they were last year. I hope you will be able to over-

come your present small difficulties and that you will be able to keep

the name at the head of your list in the front ranks.

        With best wishes for the future, I remain,

Dict. R.E.O.   Yours truly,   R. E. Olds.

OLDS' LETTER TO OMW, AUGUST 19, 1904. The first name given to the new car company was meant to call upon Olds' "good-will of the trade." It was the first name most people reckoned with the industry, and was one of the reasons Shettler and the others enlisted his person. But Olds Motor Works threatened to sue if the new company in Lansing were to use "R.E. Olds Co." because, they thought, the Olds name now belonged to them. REO was finally settled upon—a kind of compromise that allowed Olds to retain his connection with the public. Notice the last few sentences in this document, which convey the deep and real sadness of Olds at having left his father's company and then having noticed it was failing. His "best wishes for the future" are genuine. (FPML/CADL.)

GRAND TRUNK RAILROAD AND REO, c. 1905. As with the Detroit factory, one of the major preferences for location of the new REO company was that it lay next to major railroad lines for ease of shipping and receiving. Pictured, people board trains and await arriving passengers, just across from the new automobile factory. The REO smokestack, at center, was located in the coal room at the far eastern part of the plant. The Grand Trunk depot was opened January 20, 1903—the second brick passenger depot to open in the city. Though abandoned, this marquee structure still stands today as the last landmark that can be readily associated with REO. (FPML/CADL.)

REO, SANBORN, 1906. With ink still wet on the contracts, the design of automobiles and construction of the factory got underway almost immediately, in September of 1904. From

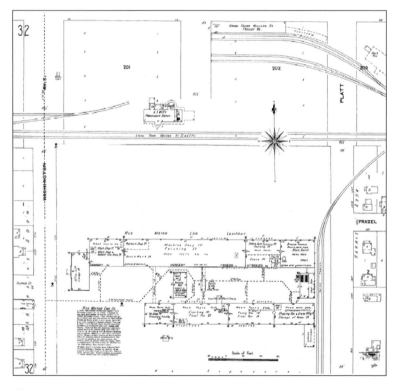

Sanborn maps we can identify most parts of a commercial structure. This one, from 1906, identifies the layout of all of the first REO buildings. The office building (facing Washington Avenue, at left) was one of the first to be built. Right to left (top), from the office building, are the machine and pattern shops, painting room, and black smith. Left to right (bottom) are shipping and storage, two assembly rooms, and the trim and finishing room.

REO OFFICE. The REO office was one of the first buildings erected because it was to serve as a multifunction facility. Before there was an engineering building, this was where all planning was done, as with accounting and human resources. This photo postcard dates to a few years after the original construction, foretold by the ivy on the façade at a semi-advanced stage. (Caterino/CADL.)

REO PLANT, c. 1908. Within 60 days of the creation of REO, Olds had his first prototype—built in a leased food plant while the factory was under construction. Perhaps because he felt he had something to prove on so many levels (to his former colleagues at OMW, to the investors of REO who were also once investors in his earlier businesses, and to his hometown), the factory and his first production automobile appeared in great speed, but also with great care. Olds himself test-drove the first prototype for 2,000 miles before giving the green light to production, which began January 1, 1905. The sign at the bottom of the plant (at left) reads: "Lansing the Great Auto Mfg City" for the benefit of those coming off trains at the Grand Trunk. (Caterino/CADL.)

THE "FINISHED" COMPLEX, c. 1920. Though some shops would be rearranged after truck production was added, this is a bird's-eye-view of what may be considered the "complete" REO factory. The test track of the previous image has been removed in favor of the clubhouse (lower right), and the engineering building stands on the other side of the office on Washington Avenue. All told, the area of the REO facilities, bounded by Washington and Cedar, Baker and the Grand Trunk Railroad, totaled 72 acres. (Caterino/CADL.)

RUNABOUT MODEL. There were two models introduced as the first REOs, though both were significantly different from Olds' signature Curved Dash model. Olds brought along Horace Thomas, his engineer from OMW, and with the urging of Shettler, REO began to work away from the horseless carriage model. They were beginning to make a product that more resembles what we now call the automobile. The differences in the two models were, especially, price— $650 and $1,250. Pictured is the Runabout model, which was the much simpler car for the masses. Under the hood was not an engine, but a gas tank, a radiator, and batteries. Also notice the child standing on a running board, another invention credited to Olds. (Caterino/CADL.)

AXEL ASSEMBLY. The next four photographs demonstrate "life on the line" at REO in the early days, *c.* 1910. Only sections of assembly lines actually moved in the days before parts were placed on a conveyor. Here workers assemble axels with parts that would have been forged and stamped in other factories around the city, then brought to REO for machining and put together by hand. (REOTM.)

MACHINE ROOM. Notice the belts and pulleys that were attached to centralized motors that turned individual machines, as also seen in the Olds Motor Works photo. Factory conditions were especially dangerous in a shop like this one, with the high risk of catching clothes and limbs in the ever-present, high-speed motors turning presses and lathes for assembly parts. (REOTM.)

MOTOR ASSEMBLY. In these factory photos, notice the amount of materials and labor that would have been the responsibility of Lansing industry outside the REO factory. The handcart that supports the motor in this photo, as well as those pictured on page 55, would probably have been manufactured by Lansing Co. (formerly Lansing Wheelbarrow), as well as the castings and bearings that make the cart easy to move when loaded. Eventually, Olds would attempt to manufacture as much needed material as possible inside the shop or in one of his satellite businesses around the city. (REOTM.)

SEAT MAKING. One of the great reasons it was possible to get REO running so quickly and efficiently (making 2,500 cars in 1906) was because Lansing supplied a pool of skilled labor. Bement, Lansing Co., Auto Wheel, and others were long in business before REO and were stocked with skilled workers. Even more importantly, because OMW had already been established, Lansing was the only city in the country with a sizable population of trained autoworkers. Here, REO workers assemble seats by hand. (REOTM.)

WOMEN IN TRIMMING DEPARTMENT. Although there are no statistics on REO for the time, the number of women in the industrial labor force in Lansing around the time of REO's founding was only 250. In 1910, before the truly great boom of auto production—between 1915 and 1925—there were 139 women working in auto factories in the entire United States. But by 1920, when the total number of workers in the city was approximately 15,000, the census records 1,101 women working in "mechanical and mechanical industries," though the figure reflects parts suppliers and body makers where most women had been previously employed. Especially true in the early years of auto manufacturing, women were employed in "traditional" ways, when they were employed at all. Here, REO women work in the Trimming Department, fashioning bolts of fabric for use in seats and other interior areas of automobiles. (Caterino/CADL.)

CAR CHASSIS. By the mid-1910s, Americans were beginning to reconcile themselves to the idea that the horseless carriage was here to stay. In 1909 the total number of automobiles made in the country was 64,800, but by 1914 the total was a comparatively astronomical 437,083— at which point sales leveled off until the great boom of the "Roaring Twenties" saw units manufactured climb to a whopping 3.5 million. Though REO's total output remained steady during the early 1910s, its market share was dramatically falling because of increased competition. Pictured are REO car chassis waiting for the addition of the final stage of production: the body. (REOTM.)

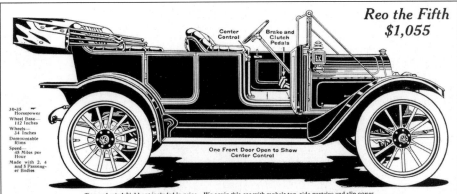

REO THE FIFTH. Displaying Olds' name prominently in the REO the Fifth ads was the first step toward reaching into the collective memory of the automobile consumer, or so thought advertising whiz Claude C. Hopkins. Sales were beginning to dip after a peak of 6,592 in 1909—partly because of an intense amount of competition from automakers that sprang up all over the nation, and partly because the company's engineering was failing to forge ahead. At the time REO was looked upon as standing still in an industry that was quickly moving forward with invention and ingenuity, and its market share was dropping. Hopkins wrote copy that looked and sounded like R.E. Olds, himself, assuring potential buyers that he was testing vehicles bumper to bumper, and that the vehicle came with his personal guarantee. The price was $1,055—a cost, the ad claimed, paired to the limit. The false claim of "farewell" was, though, to prove somewhat fortuitous, since Olds would bow out of the industry several times before his actual retirement in 1936. (OHC.)

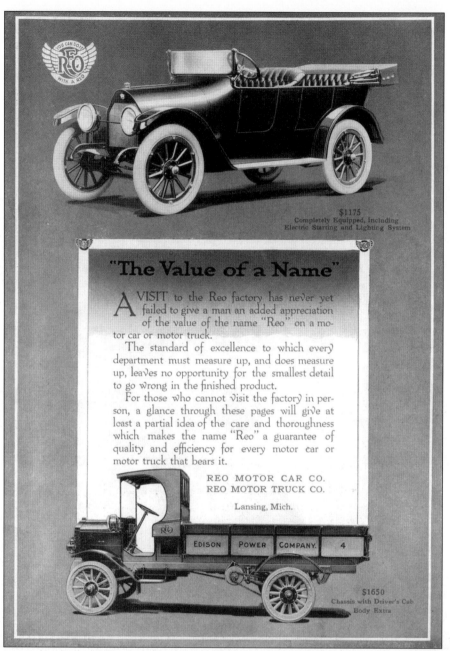

$1175
Completely Equipped, Including
Electric Starting and Lighting System

"The Value of a Name"

A VISIT to the Reo factory has never yet failed to give a man an added appreciation of the value of the name "Reo" on a motor car or motor truck.

The standard of excellence to which every department must measure up, and does measure up, leaves no opportunity for the smallest detail to go wrong in the finished product.

For those who cannot visit the factory in person, a glance through these pages will give at least a partial idea of the care and thoroughness which makes the name "Reo" a guarantee of quality and efficiency for every motor car or motor truck that bears it.

REO MOTOR CAR CO.
REO MOTOR TRUCK CO.

Lansing, Mich.

EDISON   POWER   COMPANY.   4

$1650
Chassis with Driver's Cab
Body Extra

TRUCKS. A year before REO the Fifth, Olds had purchased the old Bement factory on Grand, and began production in what was at first something like a division of REO, the REO Motor Truck Co. In the beginning, REO Truck was actually a separate company, but REO owned the majority of it, and it was managed by the same people: Olds, President; R.H. Scott, Vice President and General Manager; J. Edward Roe, Secretary; D.E. Bates, Assistant Secretary and Treasurer. It was a success from the start, pressing ahead in new directions of engineering while tapping a new commercial market. "Speed Wagons" sold nearly 1,000 in their first year, and the truck component of the REO company would go on to become an American institution. Pictured is an ad that builds on the name recognition that worked so well in the REO the Fifth campaign. (FPML/CADL.)

REO MOTOR TRUCK CO., GRAND AND IONIA. REO paid $40,000 for the vacant E. Bement & Sons (which moved to River Street before going out of business) factory at Grand and Ionia and began building trucks in 1910. Trucks were a bold move for the company at that time, and after many reorganizations in the years to come, became the sole focus of production after the Great Depression, in the 1930s. This facility was used until the South Washington Avenue factory could be expanded in 1916. (REOTM.)

SPEED WAGON AT REO. Pictured c. 1913 is an early, stripped-down Speed Wagon demonstrating what would become the company slogan, "World's Toughest Truck." We know this is the South Washington Avenue factory because of the tracks leading into the building, where there is a sign in the doorway that reads "Grand Trunk." REO would also take over the Duplex Truck factory, at Washington and Mt. Hope (next to Atlas Drop Forge), in order to expand its manufacturing facilities in 1923. (REOTM.)

BOARD OF DIRECTORS. By the time REO began to solidify its position as one of America's greatest truck manufacturers, R.E Olds was drifting toward other projects and industrial concerns—in Lansing and especially in Florida. Though Olds was still majority stockholder, by 1915 the company was being managed by R.H. Scott. Scott and Olds went back to the days of OGEW, when Olds replaced his brother, Wallace (who was floor manager at the time), with Scott when Wallace sided with labor during a dispute. Scott came to REO in 1904 and served as Superintendent and Vice President until officially gaining control in 1915. In 1916, Scott reorganized the company, merging the truck and auto companies and expanding the line of car models that had once again stagnated. Pictured is the chain of command, as it existed at the time when Olds stepped down as President and took the title of Chairman. (FPML/CADL.)

LOGO, c. 1928. R.H. Scott brought in new, outside designers who developed mid- and upper-level models that included the Flying Cloud, the Wolverine, and the Royale. These vehicles now epitomize to us the Art Deco, Roaring Twenties aesthetic, and sales figures soared in the middle and end of that decade—reaching as high as the 30,000 mark. Compare the aesthetic of this 1920s logo to that of the 1910s, on page 60.

1931 FLYING CLOUD. Perhaps the greatest of all REO eras, for design, was the end of the 1920s and the early part of the 1930s. Priced upwards of $2,000, these vehicles were far beyond the economic reach of Americans suffering through the Great Depression. To boost sales, Scott tried making more individual, specialized models, but the expansion and diversification of the auto line, coupled with internal managerial battling, the slow economy, and tough competition forced the permanent suspension of automobile manufacturing at REO for good in 1936. (REOTM.)

SOUTH WASHINGTON, c. 1918. The Downey Hotel (Charles P. Downey was an original REO investor) and Butler Block building dominate this photo of the 300 block of South Washington, c. 1918. By this time Lansing had grown from the relatively small industrial village of the 19th century to a modern American city of paved roads, trolley cars, and electric lighting—thanks in large part to the wealth of infrastructure brought in by its automobile manufacturing concerns. Between 1900 and 1920, Lansing's population grew from 16,000 to 57,000, and the city was also expanding its geographical borders to accommodate this influx. Notice the streets of the business district, now without trace of horse-drawn locomotion. (Reuther.)

Four
THE SOCIETY OF REO

R.E. OLDS AND THE MINI REO. REO was more than just a car company. A worker in "the REO Family" was an "REOite." The part of the city built in response to the housing shortage generated by the growth of automobile factories in the early 20th century—east and west of South Washington, extending down past Mt Hope—was called "REO Town." The management of the company, especially in the 1920s and 1930s, fostered this paternal "family spirit" and attempted to create a work environment that was a world unto itself. The objective was to create a sense of belonging and loyalty among the ranks, but also to ward off unionization, combat turnover, and other worker dissension. (REOTM.)

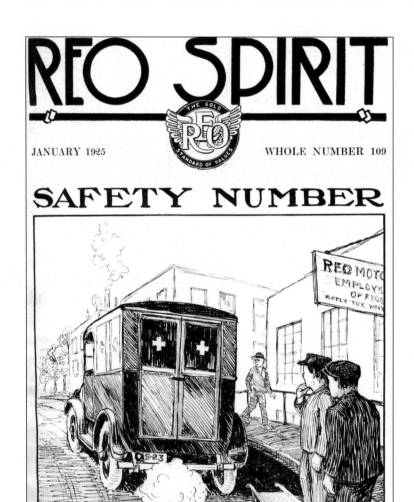

REO SPIRIT

JANUARY 1925 WHOLE NUMBER 109

SAFETY NUMBER

"PLAY SAFE"
AND RIDE IN YOUR OWN AUTOMOBILE!

REO Spirit. After the rise of the automobile, the industrial workforce of Lansing became its largest employment sector. During the turbulent labor period of the early 20th century, management of large industrial companies felt they had to be creative in stemming the tide of communism and other "lefty" organizational insurgencies that were sweeping the labor force throughout the nation. REO's answer was the creation of the Welfare Department (in 1916), which organized social and sporting activities, advised on matters of health, money management, and legal concerns. The department's outward expression was its monthly publication, the *REO Spirit.* The *Spirit* was " . . . published because the REO Family wants it published . . . ." as the slogan said. The magazine announced recreational activities and kept standings for industrial league teams, printed birth notices, provided general company news, attempted to be a "patriotic" voice for a culturally mixed workforce, and was a constant enthusiasm for proper job performance.

66

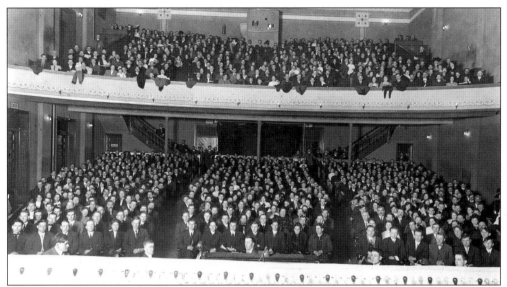

REO DAY AT THE BIJOU. This *c.* 1901 photo shows an early attempt by REO management to gather employees together in a social setting in order to foster the "togetherness" of the REO family. The idea of such an event was in part to get management and labor together in order to show they were all "on the same team." The *Spirit* often extolled the virtues of management who "spoke the shop man's language," and employees were encouraged to understand that they all worked toward the same ends—a productive company that was good for the benefit of all. The Bijou, at the corner of Michigan and Capitol, eventually burned down and became the site of the Olds Hotel. (MSUAHC.)

REO CLUBHOUSE. Dedicated in 1917, at the outset of the Welfare Department's campaign of "welfare capitalism," the REO Clubhouse was the center of social activity for the REOite, and was home to the Welfare Department. The building housed its own theater for concerts, movies, and dramatic stagings, as well as dining and other facilities for the leisure of the REO worker, during break or after a shift. Families of REOites were also encouraged to participate in these activities after work hours. (Caterino/CADL.)

REO BALL TEAM, 1913. Pictured here is the 1913 REO baseball team, champs of the city's industrial league for that year. Sporting life was something the Welfare Department thought central to its program of welfare capitalism because it was fostered health among the ranks, and brought together management and labor in "a common goal." Armedus A. Lauzun, an Assistant Superintendent, is pictured at bottom right. It is questionable how much management and the laboring workforce were integrated in these extra-curricular activities; therefore also questionable is the extent to which and how well the upper and lower echelons of the company were united "in spirit." As the photo indicates—and as is indicated throughout the monthly newsletter—management retained its supervisory position both on and off the field. (FPML/CADL.)

REO FAMILY. By the 1920s the population of Lansing was reaching toward the 60,000 mark, and REO employed over 4,500 in its expansive factory at South Washington and elsewhere throughout the city. The REO family was, indeed, the biggest in the city, and the company liked to document its sense of "oneness." This group photo, taken between the Office and Engineering buildings, was one of many taken throughout the years (though always in different locations). (Caterino/CADL.)

WREO. Begun in 1924, the WREO radio station was the first radio station in Lansing, though it soon shared the same bandwidth with WKAR. Because of its great signal, the REO family could now be extended to many states beyond Midwestern borders. Broadcast from the Clubhouse, programming included dance music on Saturday nights, all day church services Sunday, and concerts from the REO Glee Club, the REO Band and Orchestra, and the REO Male Quartet on alternating nights—Monday, Wednesday, and Friday. Bookkeeper Ray Davis was the Announcer and Program Director. Notice the odd addition of the mountain in the background of this idealized portrait of the factory. (FPML/CADL.)

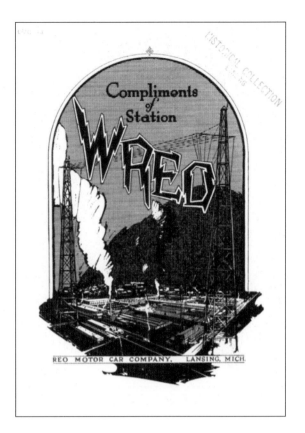

REO BAND. Carl Hall Dewey was Musical Director of the REO band, which gave its last concert in 1927. The band's duties were many and included broadcasts on WREO, parades, picnics, and concerts. A concert program, *c.* World War I, gives an example of the sequence of events for the evening: Opening Ceremony; Flag Raising; and Battle Prayer (with note that requests audience at this time to be expected "to arise, with bowed heads in silent prayer to our boys and allied cause"). Musical pieces from the evening also included Verdi, Brinquet, a song from the REO Band Quartet, something called "From Fireside to Battlefield," and ended with, of course, "The Star Spangled Banner." (FPML/CADL.)

REO ATHLETIC SHOW. Picnics were announced in the *Spirit* and held at least once per late summer in what is now Waverly Park. A full set of activities were scheduled and offered up for amusement, including the pictured "REO Athletic Show"—a test of strength that pitted a wrestler against anyone willing to try his luck in the ring for cash prizes. In this challenge, the cash amount progressed with every minute the challenger lasted. (Caterino/CADL.)

TUG OF WAR, 1913. The annual fall picnic was the benchmark social activity for the REO family, starting in the pre-Welfare Department days and lasting well into the 20th century. This photo shows another feat of strength, the tug of war, at Leadley's Park (southeast corner of Waverly and West Main)—what is now Waverly Park. Notice the roller coaster in background, and the judge for the event, a clown. (REOTM.)

REO PARADE, 1913. This is the same baseball team from page 68, lead by Lauzun, on the 100 block of South Washington. The team played and beat REO Truck on this REO Labor Day in 1913 (same day as previous photo), at Leadley's Park. Notice the storefront shops on Washington at the time. The Boston Café, at 115 South Washington, was operated by Vlahakis & Stotis. The city's Greek population has been strong since the turn of the 20th century (as in Detroit), and over the years REO employed many immigrants from the Holy Lands. (REOTM.)

REO PARADE, 1913. A parade marcher holds a sign that proclaims what part of the REO family his group represents—Lauzun's Rear & Front Axel and Steering Gear Assemblies— while the young man in the back of the truck demonstrates the "Bevel Gear Generator Driven by Our 1914 Electric Starter Motor"—apparently new wares engineered by the REO team. Notice all of the stars and stripes regalia in these photos. Part of the plan of welfare capitalism was to make workers mindful of their place in the "American patchwork"—teamwork on a much grander scale, no matter the worker's country of origin. (REOTM.)

REO WORKERS. These two group photos were taken on the eve of American involvement in World War I, on REO factory grounds. Especially noticeable in the larger group shot is what is absent from the image. Possibly due to this being a part of the factory that required skilled workers, and therefore those with experience, there are few young men. Also absent are women, who mostly worked in trimming, the office, and the soon-to-be-opened clubhouse. But notoriously absent from all early REO photos are the presence of black workers. Census statistics from 1900 indicate a small African American population in Lansing, comprising less than 3 percent of the total population, but as with Detroit, southern blacks were migrating north for work in the auto industry by the 1920s. Hard figures are not known, but given the total working Negro population to be 27,661 in Michigan in 1920, one can estimate the number of black workers in Lansing factories to be about 500 at that time. The numbers would increase dramatically after the beginning of the UAW in the 1930s (in both Detroit and Lansing), and the great insurgence of black workers to the north during World War II. (FPML/CADL.)

REO BIRD. Extending the REO family as far as possible included advertising—this is an example of one of Olds' earliest methods of "getting out the word" in demonstration of fine REO engineering. From a 1928 issue of *Spirit*, this photo was accompanied by a remembrance of Dan Wurges and the REO Bird, captured here on the old oval test ground (*c.* 1905) before the Clubhouse was built. Competing with the likes of Barney Oldfield, Wurges and the REO Bird were winning competitions all over the country, hitting speeds upwards of 90 miles an hour.

R.E. OLDS AT GARDEN OF THE GODS, *c.* 1905. Olds himself participated in the early Glidden Tours, begun by the paint tycoon and the American Automobile Association as a celebration of the durability and mechanical marvel of the early automobile. Though a fierce competition between corporate sponsors, the Glidden tours were also something of a social event for auto enthusiasts, proven by this obviously posed shot. Olds remembered well how the Whitman and Hammond trek in the Curved Dash made a reputation for OMW, and an REO ran in every Glidden tour until its end in 1913. (MSUAHC.)

WHITMAN AND HAMMOND REUNITED. In 1910 Lester Whitman and Eugene Hammond were reunited for a cross-country tour that would shatter all previous records. The trip began in New York City, in front of the R.M. Owen & Co. Motor Car Agency (Owen was the first exclusive dealer for REO), in a 30-horsepower, four-cylinder, 1911 Model R REO, on August 8, at midnight. Whitman sought to break his own record of 15 days, two hours, and 12 minutes, set in 1906 with a Franklin Model H. Three "relief drivers" were employed so that either Whitman or Hammond drove the car while the other went ahead on the overland train to meet up at rail depots. The car was stopped only to "repair road washouts, make mechanical adjustments, refuel, change tires or exchange driving teams." Only 28 machines were successful in the transcontinental journey since these two made their maiden trip in 1903. They arrived in San Francisco with a new official record time of 10 days, 15 hours, and 12 minutes. This kind of widely covered event was priceless advertisement for the REO company. (REOTM.)

REO PILOT, 1910. The same summer as Olds' participation in the Glidden Tour, the REO Mountaineer began the first-ever transcontinental round trip attempt. Nearly 10 months and 11,742 miles later, a pair of New York state drivers completed their tour, and REO was celebrated with another first. The Glidden reliability tours were quite a bit shorter—2,850-mile routes that ran through thirteen states in the South and the Midwest. Here, the REO Pilot navigates swollen streams between Roanoke and Winston Salem in 1910. (REOTM.)

GLIDDEN TOUR, 1910. Another chief purpose of the Glidden Tours and REO participation in other cross-country racing was to get vehicles out to the country so that rural populations could see the value and ingenuity of the new machines. Country folk would sometimes curse at automobile travelers with the old "Get a Horse!" but many were enormously curious. (REOTM.)

TEDDY ROOSEVELT VISIT. When R.E. Olds learned that Teddy Roosevelt would be coming to Lansing for the Semi-Centennial of the Michigan State Agricultural College, he made it his personal mission to get Roosevelt to take his first-ever automobile ride in an REO. It was another of Olds' publicity schemes to popularize and mainstream what was still considered a novelty. Olds is pictured at the wheel, and Roosevelt and MSC President Schneider are in back, en route from the Capitol, traveling down Michigan Avenue toward the college. (REOTM.)

REO ARMORED CAR. The Pentagon kept a close eye on developments in the automobile trade in the early 20th century. Especially of interest were the Glidden Tours and cross-country races because it had yet to be determined whether the car could replace rail travel as the fastest mode of delivery. REO also was a manufacturer of military machinery through the years, and like Oldsmobile and the Detroit factories, shut down commercial production completely in order to make tanks, guns, and ammunition for the Arsenal of Democracy during World War II. Pictured is an early REO armored car, *c.* 1917. (REOTM.)

"ADVANCED NATURALIZATION." Olds' world travels are well documented, and he performed philanthropic roles in foreign nations partly as a result of the connections he established while traveling. Shortly after the end of World War I, he visited Constantinople and the Holy Lands of the Near East, where the aftermath of the war led him to fund refugee relief. For his efforts, he would later receive the Cross of the Redeemer from King George II, of Greece, and was appointed Grand Knight of the Order of the Orthodox Knights of the Holy Sepulcher by the Greek Orthodox Church. The REO factory was just above 10 percent foreign born during the 1920s and 1930s, and many received their citizenship while working for the company. Pictured is the REO "Advanced Naturalization" class, another program offered by the Welfare Department, whereby immigrants would learn not only the language but also the ways of the productive American worker and how to be a good male REO role model. Cyrus Rath (standing, 1933) was the infamous labor director who for years "enforced" the REO codes of conduct, both on the job and off, through practices that would be considered horrendously unacceptable today. Workers were told, for example, to "Speak American. If You Don't Like It LEARN IT. If You Don't Like It MOVE" the *Spirit* proclaimed. The begrudging acceptance of labor unions by the administrations of all large Lansing factories in 1937 finally put an end to such "official" practices. (MSUAHC.)

REO POLICE. In 1920 the *Spirit* introduced the first uniformed patrol squad in a Lansing factory. The purpose of the patrol was not to canvas company grounds and safeguard workers against neighborhood crime, but to ensure workers were following REO protocol. Because of the intolerance of management toward absenteeism, lateness, smoking on the job, and "casual" work habits, rules of all kinds were instituted in order to bring a greater sense of uniformity and order to the workplace, and therefore boost productivity. The job of the 35-man patrol team was to keep workers in line, and if workers were caught breaking rules, they were laid off. Since profits and the value of the company increased during the time of these strict worker regulations, it is hard to say that welfare capitalism of this sort didn't work—but the cost is also not measurable. In this photo, notice how few young men were part of the squad, and the relatively advanced age of the majority. Patrolmen were paid less than those working machines in the factory. (REOTM.)

REO FACTORY, LOST ANGELES. The reach of the REO family was both national and international. Factory branches included Los Angeles, Detroit, Kansas City, Dallas, Newark, San Francisco, Chicago, Windsor, New Rochelle, Phoenix, and Brooklyn. Before the Great Depression, this factory system was behind only Ford and the companies of General Motors in terms of net worth. Though the branch factories were out of the actual reach of Cyrus Rath at the Lansing facility, there is evidence in the *Spirit* to support that the company's policies were standardized and were practiced throughout the system. (FPML/CADL.)

CAPITAL CITY AUTO. Occupying nearly the entire block of 300 East Michigan Avenue, between the train tracks and the Grand River (see page 12), Capital City Auto Co. (c. 1913, under President J. Edward Roe) sold and repaired the local product in a high-profile location. Privately owned dealerships, which paid cash on delivery of vehicles, were one of the first Olds business "inventions." REO dealerships were also another way of propagandizing the company and were in abundance throughout the U.S. This kind of high-profile, downtown dealership went the way of automobile production, though, when REO ceased manufacturing cars in 1936. (FPML/CADL.)

R.H. Scott and the REO Royale. In 1926 R.H. Scott began to diversify the line of automobiles even further, and for a time the company's sales soared. But a sales peak of nearly $60 million in 1928 was down by 1929, and Scott was removed as General Manager, though he retained the title of President. That same year REO debuted its most extravagant and expensive automobile to date, the Royale. This was beginning of the Great Depression, and timing couldn't have been worse. Pictured is William R. Wilson (Scott's replacement as General Manager), Scott, and Charles M. Toms, a Lansing banker beside what was perhaps the auto industry's worst-timed, yet greatest car. (REOTM.)

1936 REO FLYING CLOUD. The Great Depression killed off most small automobile manufacturers for good. "The Big Three" at the time dominated the market at the time and what was perceived as duplication of models made competition difficult. In the spring of 1934, a complicated and acrimonious struggle between a faction of "independent stockholders," led by R.H. Scott, attempted to wrest control of the company from Olds (still Chairman) and his backers. On April 18, the *New York Times* declared "Olds Keeps Control of REO Directorate" and noted that the independents simply "gave up the fight." (REOTM.)

FLYING CLOUD BUS. The previous photo of the 1936 Flying Cloud shows one of the last automobiles to be made by the REO company. In the same year that REO would permanently suspend manufacturing of automobiles, R.E. Olds finally retired from the REO Motor Car Company, and ended his 40-year association with the industry. Donald Bates, President after Scott, almost simultaneously announced that REO would concentrate solely on manufacturing trucks— something some historians say should have happened long before. Pictured here is a Flying Cloud bus, *c.* 1938. The company now manufactured Speed Wagons (the name is said to come either from a Lansing manufacturer of carriages and farm wagons, the Power Bros., in the 19th century, or from Frank Clark), trucks of all lines, and buses—almost exclusively for the commercial market. For a time sales did well, but by the 1940s REO Motors Inc. was having the kind of financial troubles that would plague the company through its White Motor Company days, and its final incarnation as Diamond Reo Trucks, Inc., which filed for bankruptcy May 30, 1975. (REOTM.)

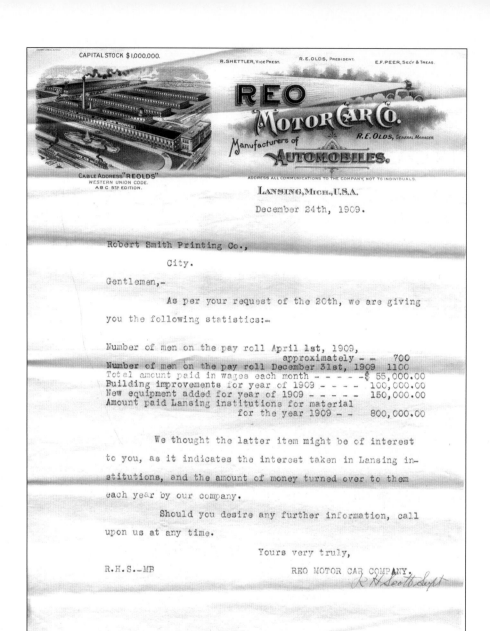

LANSING, MICH., U.S.A.

December 24th, 1909.

Robert Smith Printing Co.,

     City.

Gentlemen,—

     As per your request of the 20th, we are giving
you the following statistics:—

Number of men on the pay roll April 1st, 1909,
               approximately — —   700
Number of men on the pay roll December 31st, 1909 1100
Total amount paid in wages each month — — — — —$ 55,000.00
Building improvements for year of 1909 — — — — 100,000.00
New equipment added for year of 1909 — — — — — 150,000.00
Amount paid Lansing institutions for material
              for the year 1909 — —   800,000.00

     We thought the latter item might be of interest
to you, as it indicates the interest taken in Lansing institutions, and the amount of money turned over to them
each year by our company.

     Should you desire any further information, call
upon us at any time.

              Yours very truly,

R.H.S.—MB   REO MOTOR CAR COMPANY.

                        R H Scott Supt

SCOTT LETTER TO STATE REPUBLICAN. This 1909 letter was written in response to a State Republican request that large firms total their yearly figures for expenditures to be included in the January 1 directory for the following year. The increase in number of "men" on payroll between April and December is interesting—from 700 to 1100, as are the amount paid in wages ($55,000), building improvements ($100,000), and new equipment added ($150,000). Olds Motor Works sent in the same form, and its figures are understandably higher in human resources, but lower for building and machinery costs. What is most striking about this document, though, is the figure for "Amount paid Lansing institutions for material for the year 1909 ($800,000)." Though the figure itself is an enormous sum of money that would support many other Lansing businesses, it was Scott's act to include that sum (and the second to last paragraph) that suggests a localized REO "family" attitude that would go far in making Lansing a modern industrial city. (FPML/CADL.)

Five
INDUSTRIAL LANSING IN THE SHADOW OF OLDS

QUEEN BEE CIGAR, c. 1910. After the rise of the automobile, the city went from Capital City to Auto City. Carriage makers were all but gone, and other manufacturers were servicing Olds' former and present companies. There was also a new sense of identity in Lansing, its citizens having witnessed the transformation of their outpost-capital to status as a Midwestern industrial hub. This Queen Bee Cigar Co. advertisement, c. 1910, demonstrates civic pride in its modern city. Of note is the difference in price of cigars—the "Auto City" was 10¢, whereas the "City Hall" was 5¢. (Caterino/CADL.)

#1—SOUTH END OF GRAND RIVER, FROM MICHIGAN AVENUE. The next set of six photographs represents a full 270-degree aerial triptych of Lansing in 1912. If set end to end, they make an almost seamless panorama that demonstrates the city's industrial, geographical, and civic makeup just after the arrival of the automobile. In this shot, looking south along the Grand River, notice how closely homes were built to the factories along the river—an indication of a time before the automobile. That's Cedar running straight through middle of photo, and an iron Kalamazoo Street Bridge at right. (FPML/CADL.)

#2—THE GRAND RIVER, BETWEEN ALLEGAN AND KALAMAZOO. Dominating this view is the Bates & Edmonds Motor Co., at 238 Mill Street (bottom left to center). The tracks of the LS & MS Railway run north and south along Mill Street, through the industrial corridor on the river. The backside of John Bohnet & Co., an early, short-lived automobile maker is on Grand, across the river to the left. Also visible are landmarks on South Washington, two blocks from the river, including the easily spotted white Butler Block building, at top right. (FPML/CADL.)

#3—THE GRAND RIVER, BETWEEN MICHIGAN AND WASHTENAW. The amount of territory along the banks of the river used for freight is noticeable. Just south of the Capitol (upper right) is Allegan Street, running to the west at center. The Hollister Block (the location of the offices of many Lansing businessmen including E.W. Sparrow), and the State Building are visible at Washington Avenue (center). Fading away on Allegan, the steeples of the First Presbyterian and Plymouth Congregational churches are still visible. The Downey Hotel is the big square building upper left, at Washtenaw. (FPML/CADL.)

#4—NORTH ON THE GRAND RIVER. Cedar Street, running from the bottom of the photo north to the top, and the iron bridges of Shiawassee, a railroad bridge, Saginaw, and Franklin are distinctive in this photo. On the east side of the river, the passenger depot and freight yards of the LS & MS Railway, Michigan Condensed Milk Co. (at Shiawassee), and grounds of the Lansing Co. (long white building running parallel to Cedar and river) are discernable. At bottom left is the store of Fred W. Houghton, Druggist, at 431 East Michigan, and Postal Substation No. 2. The barn-like structure near the depot, at 402 Condit, is M.H. Hunt & Son, Bee Supplies and Berry Baskets. (FPML/CADL.)

#5—NORTH ON LARCH. Larch is the unpaved road running from right to top left. The tops of storefront shops and homes on the 500 block of Michigan Avenue are below. At center is the steepled Larch Street School. Freight yards for the Michigan Central Railroad line the corridor of East Street, at top right. At 710 East Shiawassee, at top right, International Havester is visible just above the one-story freight houses. (FPML/CADL.)

#6—NORTHEAST, MICHIGAN AVENUE. Michigan and Larch begins at bottom left. Prominent in the photo, at center, is the J.I. Case Threshing Machine Co. (which also made tractors), at 113 North East Street, and the storefront shops of Michigan Avenue (running from bottom left to upper right). Next to J.I. Case, the roof of the Michigan Central passenger depot is visible. Above Case is the Michigan Distributing Co. (a wholesaler of agricultural implements, wagons, and carriages), at 221 North Hosmer, and above that, the tops of the Victorian-style peaked roofs of the enormous Industrial School can be seen, at Shiawassee and Pennsylvania. At this time (c. 1912), the products of Case and Michigan Distributing were becoming antiquated for Lansing businesses, though notice the traffic on Michigan Avenue and the obvious lack of motor vehicles. (FPML/CADL.)

WASHINGTON AND MICHIGAN, c. EARLY 1910S. Lansing's downtown roads were ready for the automobile, the first getting brick pavement in 1894. All forms of the city's transportation are visible here in this early 1910s shot of Washington Avenue at Michigan—electric streetcar, horse-drawn wagons and carriages, and the automobile. Notice the incredible tangle of telephone and electric lines that cross above the street. The white Ingersoll Block building, home to City National Bank (E.F. Cooley, Vice President) is at left. (FPML/CADL.)

HUB OF LOWER MICHIGAN. This advertisement from the 1907 city directory shows Lansing's growing stature in the industrial marketplace. It is evidence of the attempt to beckon further outside interests away from "large cities" and into the Lansing community. Though a sponsor for the ad is not given, it is almost certainly the same group responsible for the permanent homes of Oldsmobile and REO—the Lansing Business Men's Association, which had yet to become the Chamber of Commerce. Most of the increase in commerce and industry listed for 1906 is directly an outgrowth of the automobile business. Their claim to "give fine factory sites to legitimate concerns" was nothing more than stated fact.

87

THE GRAND RIVER, c. 1910. Though the city's biggest industrial concerns (OMW and REO) built their factories in the less-populated southern part of the city in the early 20th century, the central downtown riverfront was still being developed and redeveloped for industrial concerns. At left is the relatively new facility (c. 1908) of the Michigan Power Company, where E.F. Cooley served as President. Cooley was not only an industrial giant in the city, he was also a key supplier of power. Pictured is MPC's steam plant located at 121–123 West Washtenaw. The company also produced hydroelectric power at a spot on the south part of the Grand, just across from OMW and just west of the Big Bend, at what is now Moores River Park. Notice, as well, the old train depot at right, and the Michigan Condensed Milk Co. (smokestacks at center) at the foot of the Shiawassee Street Bridge. (FPML/CADL.)

SEAGER ENGINE WORKS. The motor company that Pliny F. Olds began on River Street went through several name and site changes, before and after the automobile. After P.F. Olds & Son, it was Olds Gas Engine Works and Olds Gas Power Co. In 1909, it became Seager Engine Works when the company decided to manufacture engines for General Motors (in addition to stationary engine-making), at which time the OMW factory was expanded. For a time Seager was the name of both the River Street site as well as a site next to the OMW factory (now the Board of Water and Light). In 1915 the OMW site became Reliance Engineering, and by the early 1920s, Reliance was out of business. (Caterino/CADL.)

CLARKMOBILE. Frank G. Clark's career is an interesting study that lies in the shadow of his longtime friend and business associate, R.E. Olds. They were approximately the same age and spent teenage years at their fathers' shops on the Grand River. Clark made the bodies of the first working Olds automobiles, and was an initial investor in Olds Motor Vehicle Works. On the heels of the successes of his friend, he put together his own automotive manufacturing company and called it, naturally, Clarkmobile. He joined forces with Arthur C. Stebbins (of Lansing Wheelbarrow and Lansing Co., and a former Olds Motor Vehicle Co. Secretary), and H.E. Thomas (who was a member of the Lansing Business Men's Association, and instrumental in bringing Olds back to Lansing from Detroit), in the making of a one-cylinder runabout (pictured). Unfortunately, few buyers were lured away from the inexpensive and well-known Oldsmobile. The "Unbreakable Clarkmobile" carried the hefty price of $2,000, which was out of reach for most people in 1903—especially for a vehicle that was not yet accepted by the populace. This, however, would not be the end of Frank Clark's ventures into automobile manufacturing. (FPML/CADL.)

CLARK & CO. FACTORY FIRE. The Clark & Co. (see pages 15–16) factory, at Grand and Washtenaw, burned to the ground on July 3, 1906. Frank was the manager of the company then, and when it burned, the business his father established in 1865 passed with what was effectively the end of an era in Lansing—carriage manufacturing. Pictured is the aftermath of the fire. (FPML/CADL.)

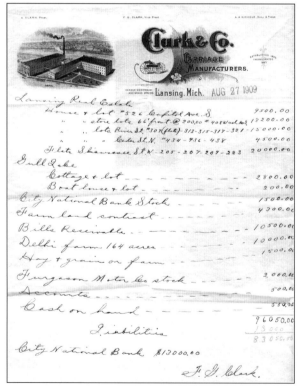

CLARK ASSETS, 1909. The stationery here may look anachronistic, since the letterhead of the note says Clark & Co., but is dated 1909. The document lists property held by Clark, including prime commercial real estate on the 400 block of South Washington (at Arbaugh's Department Store), nearly half an entire block on the 200 block of West Shiawassee, and a large cottage property at Gull Lake (south of Lansing). But most interesting is stock held in the Furgason Motor Co. Rather than remain a stockholder in Olds' companies, Clark put his money into another local manufacturer. Though there is not much known about this company, there is evidence that Claude E. Furgason, who owned a machine shop, provided Furgason its namesake before becoming manager of the Woodstock Auto Co. of Ontario, Canada. (FPML/CADL.)

FRANK CLARK AND FAMILY. Pictured are Frank G., Harriet (wife), Hannah Ellen (mother), and children, Kathleen and John Clark, at Gull Lake in 1911. The family sits aboard a Clark Superior truck. After the failure of the Clarkmobile and the fire at the family carriage shop, Frank turned his energies toward building commercial vehicles—the kind of market REO would have success with, but would prove much more difficult for smaller companies such as Clark's. (FPML/CADL.)

COLUMBIA MOTOR & TRUCK CO. Perhaps Clark was typical of those who may be considered early auto industry pioneers. His principal trait seems to have been that he wouldn't give up. R.E. Olds kept count of the number of auto manufacturers who had tried and failed by the years nearing the end of his life—approximately 1,000. This is most likely a startling figure to those of us who grew up knowing but the handful of companies that survived the Great Depression. Pictured is one of Frank Clark's last efforts, Columbia Motor & Truck, which was begun in Kalamazoo and relocated to Pontiac. It is unknown how many units the company manufactured—perhaps due to the unfortunate duplication of a company name already established elsewhere. (FPML/CADL.)

MADISON F. BATES. Another man whose career was cast in the shadows of R.E. Olds was Madison F. Bates. Also the son of an industrialist, Bates was, like Olds, an inventor from an early age. In 1893, when Ransom Olds began to win recognition for his early model automobiles and P.F. Olds was winning international acclaim for gas engines, Bates joined the shop on River Street as a mechanic. In 1898 his residence was listed as 227 River Street—right next to the Olds shop. He was instrumental in the invention of several important items for Olds, including advancements in the gasoline internal combustion engine and a two-cycle marine engine. The first outside the family to own stock in the Olds shop, he severed ties with Olds concerns in 1899 in order to join efforts with J.P. Edmonds in the Bates & Edmonds Motor Company. (REOTM.)

BATES & EDMONDS MOTOR. James P. Edmonds was the son of the first Lasing Fire Department organizer, and its first Chief Engineer. He served as City Treasurer before becoming an industrialist and co-founding Bates & Edmonds. Pictured is the kind of portable motor made by the company. The "Bull Dog" and "Bull Pup" were the models that sold by the thousands to farmers, millers, and industrialists of all kinds. (FPML/CADL.)

BATES & EDMONDS FACTORY, c. 1900. Bates & Edmonds was incorporated December 20, 1899, with a capital of $100,000. The factory was located between Mill Street and the Grand River, and at the turn of the century already employed 100 men. This is the factory that M.F. Bates left Olds to begin. Already a master engineer of the internal combustion engine, he would go on to become a "dean" of motor manufacturing in a town that was becoming a global center of the auto industry. The site is now home to The R.E. Olds Transportation Museum, on what is now called Museum Drive. (REOTM.)

BATES AUTOMOBILE CO., 1905. The Bates Automobile Co. was a splinter of the motor company Bates had with J.P. Edmonds. It was an endeavor that once again proved how difficult it was to get an automobile company into the black. In *Early Lansing History* (1944), J.P. Edmonds describes the venture as follows: "In 1902 the Bates Automobile Co. was organized by J.P. Edmonds, M.F. Bates, F.M. Seibley, J.E. Roe, and Dr. H.A. Haze. They started business in the old 'Armory' Building in the 300 block on South Capitol Avenue where the Lansing Oldsmobile is now located [*sic*]. They, at first, made a single cylinder runabout and later produced a few two-seated cars with four cylinder engines under the hood. In all, a total of about 25 cars were built." Pictured is the failed one-cylinder runabout. Some of the great differences between this model and the early Curved Dash Olds and REO runabouts are visible—especially that the engine and transmission were actually under the hood of the Bates. The motto for the car was "Buy a Bates and Keep Your Dates." (FPML/CADL.)

American
Buggy Top Co.
Manufacturers of
VEHICLE TOPS and TRIMMINGS.

TOP NOTCH
of EXCELLENCE

Jackson, Mich., Feb. 16th 04.

Bates Automobile Co.

      Lansing, Mich.

Gentlemen:

     We understand you are just starting to manufacture Automobiles.
We wish to state we make everything in Automobile tops and Automobile
trimmings. We can save you some money on this class of goods and also
give you quick service.

     Kindly let us know if you are interested, when we will be glad to
send one of our representatives to Lansing and submit figures on your
requirements.

     Trusting you will favor us with a reply by early mail, we are,

AMERICAN BUGGY TOP CO. LETTER, 1904. By the time this letter from Kalamazoo-based American Buggy Top Co. was written in 1904, the Bates Automobile Co. was just eking out production of their automobiles. One gets a sense from looking at this historical document at just how many different kinds of manufacturing concerns were chasing "trade winds" in the new industry—in hopes of being swept along with companies like Olds or REO. (FPML/CADL.)

BATES TRACTORS. Not long after the dissolve of his namesake automobile company, Bates also left his old motor shop in order to start manufacturing the new kind of agricultural implement that would completely change the world of farming—the gasoline-powered tractor. The new tractor shop was located at 700 East Franklin and was co-managed by J.A. Haze, who was also from the auto-making attempt. J.P. Edmonds stayed with Bates & Edmonds and became its President. He remained until the company became Hill Diesel when, in 1924, R.E. Olds purchased J.P. Edmonds stock. Hill made "diesel engines for marine and generator application from 12 to 60 H.P." (REOTM.)

NEW-WAY FACTORY, c. 1910. The New-Way Motor Co. was incorporated January 1, 1905, with a capital of $100,000. A.C. Stebbins—the man who was once Secretary of OMVW, Secretary and Manager of Lansing Wheelbarrow, then Lansing Co., a founder of Clarkmobile, and V.P of W.K. Prudden Co. (later Motor Wheel)—was President of the new motor manufacturer, with J.W. Knapp as Vice President and W.H. Newbrough serving as Treasurer and Manager. Early city directories listed their wares as "gasoline engines and spraying equipments," and the address as 706 Sheridan. (FPML/CADL.)

NEW-WAY CAR, 1904. For some reason, the management of the brand-new New-Way Motor Co. thought they could succeed with the Clarkmobile after it had already failed. Using leftover bodies, New-Way installed its own air-cooled motors and, it seems, sold off the remaining models. Whether or not this was a serious attempt at starting an automobile company is unknown, but it serves as a good demonstration of the maverick nature of the automobile industry in its early days. (FPML/CADL.)

NEW-WAY MOTOR. The enormous success of Olds' manufacturing of internal combustion, gasoline engines in the River Street shop led Lansing to become the central manufacturing hub of all kinds of stationary and portable motors of these kinds. As Edmonds puts it in *Early Lansing History*, "Gasoline was literally in the air." He notes that most of these companies were formed at the peak of the River Street shop until just after the arrival of the automobile, between 1895 and 1910, and their popularity was such that "thousands upon thousands were produced and shipped to every state in the Union and exported to every civilized country on the globe." New-Way produced these kinds of machines until going out of business in 1938. (FPML/CADL.)

AUTO BODY. With 600,000 square feet of floor space at 207 East Franklin, the Auto Body Co. dominated what is now called "Old Town," between the east bank of the river, west of Turner, and on the north side of what is now Grand River Avenue. Its management was comprised of area automobile aristocracy in the early days: H.E. Thomas, Vice President (former LBMA member); Lawrence Price, President (original investor in REO, President of Hildreth, Peerless, and Lansing Brewing Co.); and E.S. Porter, Treasurer (former Manager of Lansing Spoke and original investor in REO). Begun in 1901, it was a major supplier of car and truck bodies. (Caterino/CADL.)

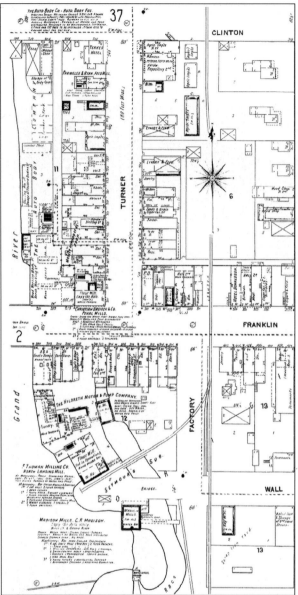

TURNER AND FRANKLIN, SANBORN, 1906. Though its shops and art galleries characterize what is now referred to as Old Town, it was once a concentrated center of industry at the turn of the 20th century, and for many years before. This Sanborn map from 1906 shows detail of the Auto Body Co. factory just north of Franklin, the mills south of Franklin, and in between the Hildreth Motor & Pump Co.—what would become Novo Engine, and another manufacturing giant of the gasoline motor. Between 1890 and 1911, the name of this company would change five times. Started as a small repair shop known as Cady & North, it became Cady & Hildreth, Hildreth & Son, Hildreth Motor & Pump Co., and Hildreth Manufacturing before becoming Novo. In the early days, the company manufactured farm pumps and marine engines of 1, 2, 3, and cylinders, then underwent a management change and moved to a location on Sheridan that brought in familiar names in Lansing manufacturing. In this map, note the mixture and close proximity of residences, shops, and industry around Turner Street.

NOVO FACTORY, c. 1913. Clarence E. Bement, Lawrence Price, E.F. Peer, Donald Bates, and R.H. Scott were all management of Novo at one time or another. Other than Bement (who started in his father's factory), all were ground-floor REO people. Manufacturers of "stationary gasoline engines and gray iron castings," this company's product line expanded throughout the years to include the largest kinds of industrial equipment. Pictured is the shop in 1912, after it moved to Sheridan Avenue, along the rail lines of the Michigan Central and next to Auto Wheel. (REOTM.)

NOVO AD. The backbone of the Novo Company in the early days was its Type S, vertical, four-cycle hopper that was used mainly for cement and mortar mixing. Over 100,000 of these models were produced and, with increased power added over the years they helped the construction industry in the building up of American cities before the Great Depression in their use as hoists. As with agricultural tools manufactured for use in the opening of the American West, Lansing-made products were once again helping to shape the American landscape. (Caterino/CADL.)

NOVO LADIES, c. LATE 1910S. Outside the Novo factory, along the tracks of the MCRR, the women of Novo send off another heavy-duty hoist to its construction-site destination. Pictured are (from left to right) Doris Winandy, Doris Tobias, M.E. Allen, Sarah Russell, Emily Anderson, Kathryn Murphy, Viola Schuller, Norma Jean Reed, and Dorathy Majchenzak. Women were most frequently employed in Lansing manufacturing in supplier companies for the auto industry, and it would not be until World War II that they took a place "on the line" in significant numbers. FPML/CADL.)

PEERLESS MOTOR CO., 1912. Incorporated September 9, 1903, with capital of $100,000, Peerless also joined the fray of motor manufacturing in North Lansing (at 1300 Turner) after the success of the Olds shop. The company President, Lawrence Price, was also an original REO investor and member of the Lansing Business Men's Association that brought OMW back to Lansing from Detroit. A former Police Chief and Marshal for the city, Price was centrally involved in most industrial concerns in the early part of the century in what we now refer to as Old Town. The motto for the company, which boasted Lansing as the "gas and gasoline city of the world" was: "There are others, but none so good." (REOTM.)

MICHIGAN RUBBER REPAIR, c. EARLY 1910S. The service industry for automobiles was also something created by Olds when, early on, he realized that if everyone with a problem came directly to the factory for service and parts, there would never be time to manufacture cars. His answer was to create the autonomous dealership, which in turn created the independent repair garage. Consider the amount of attention, in general, automobiles required vs. horse maintenance. By 1920, the Lansing city directory featured a full three and one-half pages of listings of all kinds in the automotive-related businesses, whereas in the days immediately before the automobile there were approximately 10 listings for liveries and carriage businesses. This is partly reflective of a burgeoning population, and in the 1920 city directory there are over 100 listings in the Lansing directory for automobile accessories, electric supplies and repairs, body manufacturers, hood and fender repairing, automobile manufacturers (just two at the time), painting and trim companies, radiator repair, sales agents, service stations, tire dealers and repairs, tops, seat covers and cushion makers, trailer dealers, truck bodies and truck manufacturers, wheel manufacturers, and windshield repair. Pictured is the Michigan Rubber Repair Co. (Vernon E. Lundy, Proprietor), which existed at several locations over time: South Grand, East Allegan, then two different shops on the 300 Block of South Capitol between 1908 and 1921. Tires, in those days, were like giant versions of the bicycle tires we know today— filled with inner tubes (on the floor and rack in photo), and needed constant attention given the shape of most roads. (FPML/CADL.)

DURANT MOTOR CO. PLANT. Automobile and truck manufacturing in Lansing did not stop with the early small companies and the giants of Oldsmobile and REO. In addition to all the General Motors models made in the city through the years, there were also the major concerns of Duplex Tuck and Durant Motor Car Co. After William Durant's second loss of control of General Motors, he returned in 1920 with the Durant Motor Co. The Lansing factory was built on what is now VerLinden Avenue, (Edward VerLinden, formerly of Oldsmobile, was its first factory manager,) and contributed to the city's swelling auto worker population, which reached over 13,000. (Caterino/CADL.)

STAR SIXES, 1927. The Great Depression swallowed Durant Motor Company as well as so many others, and the company was in receivership by 1932. In 1936 Fisher Body bought the factory and has been manufacturing in this spot since. Pictured is a row of Star Sixes ready to roll at the VerLinden plant, 1927. Slogans across the windshields read: "Most for the Money," "Superior Quality," and "Power." (FPML/CADL.)

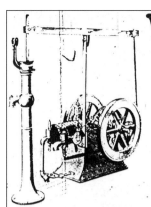

W.S. OLDS. R.E. Olds' brother, Wallace, was the first "Son" in P.F. Olds & Son, but sold his stock to his younger brother shortly after Ransom started working in the shop. Wallace stayed on as a manager until he was fired for siding with workers in 1898 and replaced with R.H. Scott. He then took his considerable motor manufacturing experience and started his own company, W.S. Olds Motor Works (as well as Air-Cooled Motor Co.) The shop was located on the 500 block of South Hosmer, where a new industrial corridor would also include future projects of R.E. Olds. (FPML/CADL.)

NATIONAL COIL LETTER, 1904.
Olds' industrial reach in the Lansing area did not stop with the manufacture of automobiles. With the incorporation of National Coil Co. in 1903 (Olds President, Cooley Vice President) he began a series of independent shops that could produce technologies on which he already held patents or was in the process of developing. The first National Coil shop was at 420–422 East Michigan Avenue, and then moved (when Olds sold control to R.H. Scott) to the old Maud S. Windmill and Pump site, at 221–223 North Cedar. This letter recruits interest in their product, electrical related motor parts, from Bates & Edmonds with the "extreme" discount of 10 percent. (FPML/CADL.)

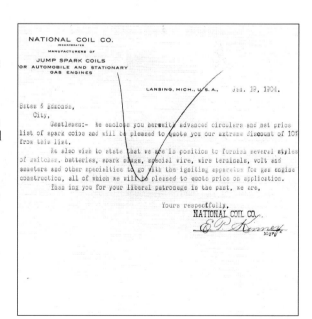

MICHIGAN SCREW CO., 1913. As the story goes, one day while walking the shop floor at REO, Olds witnessed a work slowdown because a local parts manufacturer was tardy in its shipment because it was busy making parts for other businesses. In response Olds began to assemble a network of satellite companies that would assure there was never a slowdown in production of automobiles because of a supplier. Michigan Screw was incorporated in 1906 and was located at 502 South Hosmer. "Screw machine products and automobile supplies" were its products, and its management was R.E. Olds (President) and R.H. Scott, Vice President. (REOTM.)

ATLAS DROP FORGE, 1913. Incorporated almost simultaneously with Michigan Screw, Atlas was also run by R.E. Olds, President, and first located next to the Bates & Edmonds Co., at 239 Mill, before moving to its more permanent location at Mt. Hope and Washington (now Atmosphere Annealing). Olds' creation of satellite companies was something Henry Ford would pick up on in the creation of his Rouge plant, in Dearborn, whereby an auto maker could be responsible for every component of a car's manufacture—starting with the milling and forging of steel. These companies could also take on outside jobs and remain solvent when work in auto making slowed. (REOTM.)

HILL DIESEL. In 1924 Ransom Olds bought J.P. Edmond's stock in Bates & Edmonds and started Hill Diesel in the Mill Street location. Much like Novo, the company made "diesel engines for marine and generator application from 12 to 60 H.P." The property was eventually purchased by Rogers Diesel & Aircraft (operators of Indian Motorcycle Co.) in 1941. There was a second plant for Hill, located in the old Ideal Engine factory, near Michigan Screw, at 704 East Kalamazoo, that operated until 1953. Pictured are large and small cranks in a photo demonstration of the different sizes of machinery for which the shop manufactured. (FPML/CADL.)

ORIGINAL GAS ENGINE CO., 1913. Olds was President and E.F. Cooley Vice President of The Original Gas Engine Co. For Olds, it was a return to a company like his first on River Street. The company was short-lived, though, becoming Ideal Engine Co., and then Ideal Power Lawn Co. (Cooley was Vice President throughout). In 1913 Olds was President of REO, REO Truck, Capital National Bank, Atlas Drop Forge, Michigan Screw, and R.E. Olds Co. (bonds and mortgages at time, though this would last for years as the managers of all Olds' interests). This was also a time when Olds became interested in ventures in other parts of the country. (REOTM.)

IDEAL, c. MID-1910s. The first Ideal was at 504 South Hosmer, then relocated as Original in 1912 and moved to 704 E. Kalamazoo. The company started by making motors but soon turned to the production of power lawn mowers—something Olds had been working on and received a patent for in 1915. In 1914 the company became Ideal Power Lawn Mower, and then split again in 1916, resurrecting the Ideal Engine Co. name. (REOTM.)

IDEAL AD. After Olds left the company, REO also began its own lawn mower division in 1945, with personnel from Ideal Power Mower. Its slogan was "It's more fun to mow with a REO." Consider the many uses of the internal combustion engine that were only beginning to be realized after the coming of the automobile at the turn of the 20th century. Machines for agrarian life and farm maintenance were something both Olds and Henry Ford explored fully in the period up to the 1920s. Pictured is an ad from Ideal Power Mower, which makes obvious their intended use for large-scale applications (like cemeteries and golf courses). (Caterino/CADL.)

OLDS ON MOWER, AT CAPITAL. R.E. Olds is pictured on one of his many inventions, the self-propelled power mower, in front of the Michigan State Capital, *c.* mid-1920s. (The cornerstone of the building signifies the groundbreaking and dedication dates, though both are off by a year.) Of Olds' 34 patents filed between 1880 and 1950 with the United States Patent Office, many saw immediate and lasting production and impact in the Lansing industrial trade. His patents include advancements in steam, diesel and gasoline engines, electric ignitions, tires, clutches, carburetors, motor cooling, brakes, vehicle bodies (including the convertible), tractors, and lawn mowers—not to mention advancements in manufacturing processes and the impact of factory work on those who worked in related industries. (MSUAHC.)

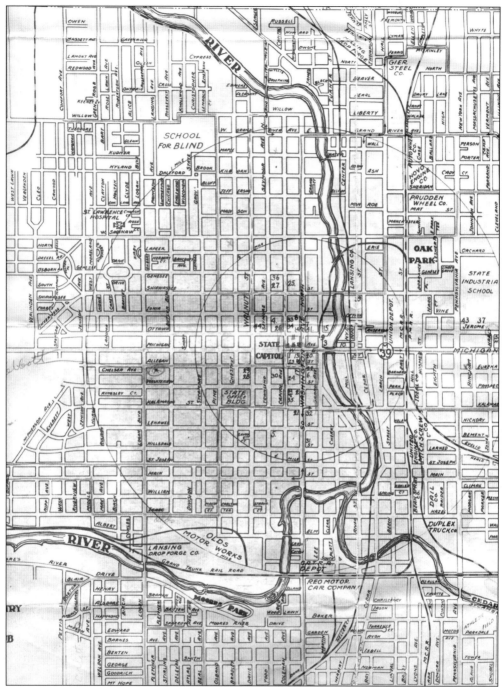

INDUSTRIAL MAP, 1927. This map from 1927 captures the city center and proximity of manufacturing companies at that time. Only the Lansing Co. remains on the river; all others have moved closer in proximity to rail lines. With the creation of the new Union Depot on Michigan Avenue, the city's main rail service now operated along this eastern industrial corridor, which included stops at the Hosmer locations, as well as the northern corridor of Novo, Prudden, and Auto Wheel, and the steel plants near North Street. (FPML/CADL.)

Six
OLDS AND COMMUNITY

720 SOUTH WASHINGTON. In 1902 the Everett House hotel, formerly Benton House and the location of two of the city's first hotels, was razed for the construction of Olds' Victorian mansion. At the time, Olds was returning from Detroit and the site was chosen, Olds said, because Washington Avenue was a paved road. The family lived at 217 South Capitol until the mansion was completed in 1904 at a cost of $25,000. (FPML/CADL.)

DARIUS B. MOON, ARCHITECT. D.B. Moon, of Moon & Spice, was the designer of the Olds mansion, as well as architect of just about everything during the great influx of population and industry at the turn of the 20th century. His projects included the residences of Hugh Lyons, Frank Dodge, E.W. Sparrow, M.F. Bates, Arthur C. Stebbins, and many others. He was also responsible for many commercial properties, including the new factory of Olds Motor Works, Sparrow Hospital, and many banks, schools, theaters, offices, and stores. His office was located in the Dodge Building, at 200 North Washington. (FPML/CADL.)

MANSION COMPLETED, 1904. The area around the Olds mansion at the time it was built was one of the more exclusive neighborhoods in the city, though the properties were not expansive and would be considered humble by the standards of today's leading industrialists. The 700 block of South Washington was just beneath the city's cosmopolitan storefront shopping district, and for years the Olds home was on the way from the city center to the REO factory. (FPML/CADL.)

720 SOUTH WASHINGTON ENTRY. The mansion was constructed of brick and sandstone, stood three and one half stories, had three fireplaces, four large family bedrooms, and five guest bedrooms. There was a ballroom on the third floor and the house was fitted with hollow tubes that acted as an intercom. Inventories of the Olds estate list his value in 1899 as $114,825, but at the time of the liquidation of his stock in OMW his value jumped to $473,600. (REOTM.)

720 SOUTH WASHINGTON MUSIC ROOM. Music and singing were an important part of Olds family activities, as the full pipe organ in this photo of the music room suggests. Visitors to the Olds family have recalled in a number of instances the Olds' predilection toward activities of all kinds, and in almost constant manner. Singing, games of all varieties, and outdoor recreation were the hallmark of the Olds' social life—whether in the Lansing home, at their northern retreat in Charlevoix, or at their southern home in Daytona Beach. (REOTM.)

720 SOUTH WASHINGTON LIBRARY. The Olds family is pictured in the library of the mansion at 720 South Washington. From left to right are Metta, Gladys, R.E., and Bernice. Gladys was born in 1892 and Bernice in 1894. The family remained a tight-knit unit in the Lansing area for most of their lives, and even after the death of R.E. in 1950, the family continued to run the financial interests of the R.E. Olds Company in the Olds Tower at Capitol and Michigan Avenue. (Gladys Olds Anderson.)

RAZING OF 720 SOUTH WASHINGTON. R.E. and Metta Olds both died within a week of one another in 1950. By the mid-1960s, the increased role of the automobile—both as means of travel within the city and throughout the world (as well as the role of the city as Michigan's Capital)—pushed urban planning in Lansing and the Tri-County area to levels not fathomed in previous planning years. The city's population was climbing toward 140,000, and to alleviate traffic concerns, as well as to better bring travelers to the city's center, an expressway was planned that would cut straight through the city's near south side—and would call for the demolition of the home of its most famous resident. Fittingly (though some say ironically), the expressway would be called the Olds Expressway. (FPML/CADL.)

PINE LAKE COTTAGE. The Olds family always enjoyed summer homes, even before the automobile made them wealthy. Pictured is the Pine Lake (now Lake Lansing) cabin owned by Pliny and Sarah. R.E. would build up this property and continue visiting the spot until he donated it to the YWCA, which renamed it Camp Matta Miga. Pictured are Pliny, his brother, Eli Olds, and Sarah on the porch of the cottage, *c.* mid-1890s. (Gladys Olds Anderson.)

ELBAMAR. Built in the mid-1910s on a community island downriver from Detroit, Elbamar, on Grosse Ile, was a much larger and more extravagant home than the house at 720 South Washington. It was a place where Olds could foster his lifetime love of yachting, and where the family would entertain in the summer months before building the home in Charlevoix. Testing for Ideal power mowers and farming experimentation for property he owned in Florida could also be conducted on the extensive property. He gave the estate to the USO during World War II, and it later became an apartment building. Pictured is the rear of the house, facing the Detroit River, upon the opening of the property to the USO. (Reuther.)

FLORIDA YACHTING, JANUARY 24, 1906. Florida was fast becoming an obsession with Olds in the years immediately following the creation of REO. He moved Pliny and Sarah there (after first going to San Diego) for their retirement, and he visited often before settling a winter residence in Daytona for himself. This photo combines many of Olds' lifetime passions: yachting, entertaining, family, and Florida. Olds is in center of photo wearing his trademark bowler hat and holding a camera. (MSUAHC.)

OLDSMAR, FLORIDA. Oldsmar was the product of R.E.'s vision of converting largely undeveloped Florida real estate in Hillsborough and Pinellas Counties into a self-sustaining worker community that had all the amenities for tourism. In 1916 Olds purchased the land through selling a Chicago apartment house, securities, and putting up approximately $200,000 cash. The 37,541 acres were developed by the new R.E. Olds Farms (Lansing office) and given the name Oldsmar. Pictured is the result of early clearing of the territory (and the work of a gas motor harnessed for a saw mill) for bungalow communities, farms, and businesses. (MSUAHC.)

OLDSMAR, FLORIDA. Olds had hoped to create a sustainable town through the local possibilities of farming, milling, tourism, and industry. A tractor factory, wood mills, and a small central downtown with a resort were established, but without the larger shipyards he hoped to secure—either from the government during World War I or in privately-controlled companies that would supply the kind of rapid influx of income that were necessary to get an entire town running—the project would fail. After the war, the country suffered an economic depression and few people, and fewer industries, moved to Oldsmar. (REOTM.)

FORT HARRISON HOTEL, FLORIDA. By the mid-1920s Olds was cutting his considerable losses in Oldsmar, and in a trade for a racetrack he was building there, acquired the Fort Harrison Hotel, in Clearwater. He also acquired the Bellerive Hotel in Kansas City, but sold that hotel in 1930 upon building Hotel Olds in Lansing. All were considered to be their city's finest at the time of his ownership. The Church of Scientology now owns the Fort Harrison, pictured here. (Caterino/CADL.)

SEA BREEZE, FLORIDA. Florida was also home to another of Olds' vacation retreats, in Sea Breeze (now Daytona). In the very early years of the 20th century, Olds found the hard-packed sand on the beaches of the area to be perfect for speed trials (as did Ford, later), and he bought a house there in 1905 (pictured), which he would visit for the rest of his life. Daytona was perhaps more important, though, for one of Olds' charities. In 1942, he purchased the Daytona Terrace Hotel, renamed Olds Hall, and converted it into a home of convalescence for ministers of all denominations. (Gladys Olds Anderson.)

LANSING WOMEN'S CLUB HOUSE. Metta Olds was also involved in several philanthropic activities. In 1909 the Olds built a clubhouse for the Ladies Library and Literary Club of Lansing at 603 South Washington, just a block north of their home. Though it opened in 1914, the structure burned in March of 1920, and the Olds rebuilt and reopened what is now the current structure shortly after. The building fell into disrepair in the years after the death of the Olds, but has been refurbished and now is occupied by the Michigan Retailers Association. (FPML/CADL.)

OLDS HALL, MICHIGAN STATE UNIVERSITY. In the 1880s, Pliny Olds secured a kind of financial bail-out loan from then President of Michigan State College, Robert C. Kedzie, when the motor shop was in economic trouble. In 1916, fire destroyed what was then the classroom building and shops for the engineering division of the school, which was at that moment thought to be in danger of transfer by the Michigan legislature to the University of Michigan. Robert Kedzie's son, Frank A., was President at the time and immediately contacted Olds, who just as quickly responded with a donation of $100,000. The gesture served as a great endorsement of the engineering school and its program was saved for generations to come. Perhaps even more important, though, is that Olds' private gift was the college's first, and thus set the precedent for sizable donations from sources other than the state government, which have contributed to the growth of the college's facilities and operations since. Olds also served on the Board of Trustees for Kalamazoo College (a Baptist-affiliated school), which gave him an honorary Doctor of Science and named the R.E. Olds Science Hall after him. Olds also served on the governing board of Hillsdale College (another Baptist school which received his donations), and Metta served on Board of Governors at Storer College for Negroes, in Virginia. R.E. Olds was a high school dropout. (FPML/CADL.)

Dedication
of
The R. E. Olds Hall of Engineering
and the
New Engineering Shops

Michigan Agricultural College
June 1, 1917

Sparrow Hospital. Edward W. Sparrow was a Lansing tycoon from upper Michigan mining and real estate concerns when Olds came seeking his financial backing to make automobiles in 1897. Sparrow was also a banker—President of City National Bank. He remained a longtime associate of Olds', long after R.E. left OMW and started REO, and Sparrow even began more industrial concerns with Olds (including National Coil). In 1910 Sparrow donated $100,000 for the construction of a hospital, and it opened in 1912. But the Olds were connected with this project more deeply than their association to Sparrow—R.E. sat on the hospital's Board of Directors from 1910 until his death in 1950, and Metta was long involved with the Women's Hospital Board, which directed medical education for early Lansing hospitals. (FPML/CADL.)

LANSING YMCA. Olds' donation of the Pine Lake property to the YWCA has already been discussed. But there is also a strong connection to the YMCA. In the 1940s, Olds held the mortgage on what was then an aging building for the YMCA. When approached for assistance in attaining a new Lansing facility for the organization, Olds cancelled the existing mortgage and made a substantial gift toward building a new one. Though a brand-new facility has recently been opened on Washington Avenue (in 2002), the former building served the community well for 50-odd years. (Caterino/CADL.)

FIRST BAPTIST CHURCH, LANSING. At 235 North Capitol, the First Baptist Church of Lansing was the most consistent beneficiary of Olds' philanthropy. Though Olds wasn't much of a churchgoer in his earlier years, he joined the First Baptist in 1912 (most likely at the urging of Metta), and the organization showed its gratitude for their newest, most wealthy member by almost immediately installing him onto the Board of Directors. His constant financial backing of the church is obvious by the fact that after his death in 1950, the church's days were numbered. It is said that Olds gave $1,000 to the construction of any church in the city, no matter the denomination. (Caterino/CADL.)

OAKLAND BUILDING. The Oakland Building was best known as home to one of Lansing's finest theaters. Called the Regent for a short time, and the Bijou for a much longer period before, the building burned December 30, 1923. It was located at the prime real estate address of 125 West Michigan Avenue, just across the street from the Capitol. By June 14, 1926, the site had been made into what would become the city's preeminent hotel, Hotel Olds (or Olds Hotel). (Caterino/CADL.)

HOTEL OLDS. Under the direction of George Crocker, the construction of Hotel Olds took nearly two years, and when it opened was immediately considered the city's foremost hotel because of its expansive amenities and convenient location in town—right across the street from the Capitol building. Its outward appearance matched that of the Prudden Building, just to the east on Michigan Avenue, with its red brick and sandstone trim. (Caterino/CADL.)

CAPITAL NATIONAL BANK. Other industrialists of the city, including Sparrow, Cooley, R.H. Scott, Prudden, and Peer were also heads of local banks when Olds started up Capital National Bank (pictured) in 1906 and was "elected" President. Its first location was in the building at 122 South Washington (though Olds' office was in the Hollister building) until Olds secured the land next to his hotel for the construction of a 26-story tower—called Capital National Bank Tower when it opened in 1931. The bank, however, failed in the Great Depression and the office building was renamed Olds Tower shortly after. (Caterino/CADL.)

OLDS TOWER. Though Capital National Bank had failed, Olds kept his financial management firm and the offices of R.E. Olds Company on the tenth floor of Olds Tower throughout the rest of his life, and the offices are still running in this location. The multicolored, Romanesque brick tower contains over 100,000 square feet of office space, and when built was the tallest building between Detroit and Chicago. Renamed Michigan National Tower (for the bank) when purchased in 1954, it is without a formal name today, though many still call it by its builder. (Caterino/CADL.)

AERIAL. It is said that a full 90% of the labor and materials used in the construction of Olds Tower came from Lansing area resources, and its 345-foot stature stands as something of a reminder of how much of the city's industrial and entrepreneurial history is tied to the man who started Oldsmobile, REO, and so many other local institutions. Because of the efforts of Lansing's early industrial pioneers and the continued effort to retain industry, over one quarter of the total 235,000 labor force of the area is still tied to manufacturing. Pictured are the Capital grounds in the 1950s, with Hotel Olds and tallest building in the city across the street. (Caterino/CADL.)

NIGHT SHOT, MICHIGAN AVENUE. By the 1970s Hotel Olds had gone through several name and management turnovers, and the building was "feeling its age." Eventually it was completely remodeled and now is known as the Romney Building—an office building that houses many official government residences. The photograph looks east from the Capitol, down Michigan Avenue *c.* 1950. (FPML/CADL.)

GOLDEN JUBILEE, 1946. Pictured are the three who would be "first" in Michigan: gas horseless carriage inventors Charles King, R.E. Olds, and Henry Ford, at the Golden Jubilee celebration in Detroit, 1946. The event marked the 50th anniversary of the arrival of the gasoline automobile and celebrated its most important pioneers. There was an accompanying parade which coincided with the 150-year anniversary of the city and brought out 1.5 million people. In attendance the night of the banquet were also Edgar Apperson, Frank Duryea, Charles W. Nash, and William C. Durant. The keynote speaker that evening was the President of the Automobile Manufacturers Association, George W. Mason, who remarked on the impact of the industry in its first 50 years: "Epochal changes have broadened the life for all, leaving in their trail a new economy and social order that has enriched the daily life of every man, woman, and child." Just how much relative influence early investors and industrial entrepreneurs have had over the sweeping transformation of the modern world is a constant topic of debate for scholars and armchair enthusiasts. An even more puzzling question might be to ask: What would the career of R.E. Olds have been if he had stayed in Detroit? And, then, what would Lansing be now? What Henry Ford has meant to Detroit (and especially to Dearborn), R.E. Olds has meant and continues to mean to Lansing. Even though his interest in automobile and truck manufacturing in Lansing waned in his later years, Olds' secondary industries continued to profoundly impact the direction and economy of Lansing. (Reuther.)

MODERN LANSING. Downtown Lansing is pictured, with the original Oldsmobile factory location to the south (top left of photo), on the banks of the Grand River in the days before the expansion of government buildings to the west of the Capitol. The tri-county area's labor force continues to be divided almost evenly between those who work in government and automobile-related industries. The impact of what began with Oldsmobile and REO has come to mean that the city is still luring auto manufacturing to the area. With the addition of the new $560 million General Motors plant—just west of the original OMW plant—and another plant in Delta Township, Lansing is the first U.S. city to open new factories in more than a decade. Though the city closes the curtains on the Oldsmobile nameplate in 2004, it also celebrates new jobs and untold millions in tax revenues for years to come. Also to be celebrated in 2004 is the REO Centennial, which promises a retrospective of Lansing-area transportation history and the legacy of automobile making and industry in the Capital City. (Reuther.)

MAP OF HISTORICAL LANSING BUSINESSES DISCUSSED IN THIS BOOK. (Courtesy of David Pfaff.)

MAP KEY

Corresponding Map Locations in Brackets

Atlas Drop Forge. First at 239 Mill [42], then S. Washington and Mt. Hope [68].
Auto Body. 207 E. Franklin (now Grand River) [19].
Auto Wheel. 637 E. Franklin (now Grand River). Later Motor Wheel [13].
Bates & Edmonds. 238 Mill [48].
Bates Tractor. 700 E. Franklin [21].
Bement, E. & Sons. Grand between Shiawassee and Ottawa [35].
Capital National Bank. Several locations: 120–122 S. Washington [48], then Olds Tower [48].
Clark & Co. (and Clarkmobile). N.E. corner Grand and Washtenaw [48].
Durant Motor Co. (Star). 401 VerLinden Ave [32].
First Baptist Church. 235 N. Capitol [41].
Fisher Body. VerLinden Ave, between W. Michigan and Saginaw [32].
Hildreth Motor & Pump. Started 1131 Race [13].
Hill Diesel. 238 Mill, then 704 E. Kalamazoo [55].
Ideal Engine Co. 504 S. Hosmer, then 704 E. Kalamazoo [55].
Ideal Power Lawn Mower. 704 E. Kalamazoo [55].
Lansing Brewing Co. 1301–1307 Turner [13] .
Lansing Iron & Engine Works. Corner Shiawassee and Cedar [42].
Lansing Spoke. 1000 N. Larch, then 1508 N. Larch [14].
Lansing Sugar Co. (Owosso Sugar Co.) 300 W. North.
Lansing Wagon Works. Grand between Shiawassee and Saginaw [35].
Lansing Wheelbarrow (Lansing Co.) S.W. Corner of Cedar and Saginaw [35].
Lyons, Hugh & Co. 100–113 E. Ottawa [42] and 700 E. South [61].
Michigan Screw. 502/506 S. Hosmer [55].
Michigan Power Co. 121–123 W. Washtenaw [48]; also 215 E. Ottawa [48], and on Grand (now Moores Park) [60].
National Coil Co. First at 420–422 E. Michigan Ave, then at 221–223 N. Cedar (now site of Oldsmobile Park) [43].
New-Way. 706 Sheridan [37].
Novo Engine Co. Several locations, last office address 702 Porter [21].
Oakland Building. Michigan and Capitol (Olds Hotel) [41].
Olds Expressway (east and west along Main Street)
Olds Hall. MSC, now Michigan State University. West Circle Drive.
Olds Hotel (now Romney Building). 111 S. Capitol [48].
Olds Motor Works. Jefferson Ave location in Detroit, then S. of Main, E. of Logan (now MLK) [60].
Olds, P.F. & Son, and Olds Gas Engine Works. 221 River Street (on site is monument) [54].

Olds Tower (Capital National Bank). 124 Allegan [48].

Olds, R.E. home. Mansion at 720 S. Washington (now Olds Expressway) [54]. Other homes at 216 E. Kalamazoo before, and 217 S. Capitol while mansion built.

Oldsmobile. Includes six plants: Plant #1 is original—S. of Main, E. of MLK [60]. Plant #2 ("Olds Forge") at 2801 W. Saginaw [32]. Plant #3 ("Jet Plant") at 2800 W. Saginaw [24]. Plant #4 (parts warehouse) at 4400 W. Mt. Hope [60]. Plant #5 (Delta Engine, GM Powertrain) at 2901 Canal Rd. [58]. Plant #6 (Fisher Body) at 401 VerLinden [32].

Original Gas Engine Co. 704 E. Kalamazoo [55].

Peerless Motor Co. 1300 Turner [13].

Prudden, W.K. Co. 701 May [29] and later 701 E. Saginaw. Later Motor Wheel [29].

R.E. Olds Transportation Museum. 240 Museum Drive [48].

REO Clubhouse. Just S. of Grand Trunk train tracks, on S. Washington.

REO factory. Bordered by Grand Trunk track to N., Baker to S., S. Washington to West, Cedar to E [62].

REO Motor Truck. First at Bement factory, Grand and Ionia [42], then at REO factory on S. Washington [62].

Schneider, J.C. & Sons. 112–114 E. Shiawassee [34].

Seager Engine. On sites of P.F. Olds & Son [54] and current location of Lansing Board of Water & Light next to Oldsmobile Plant #1 [60].

Sparrow Hospital. 1215 E. Michigan Ave [38].

Stevens Artificial Stone. Michigan Ave, just E. of bridge, N. side of street [42].

Thoman Milling. South of Franklin (now Grand River), next to River [13].

Women's Club. 603 S. Washington [54].

YMCA. 603 W. Lenawee St [53].

BIBLIOGRAPHY

Anderson, Gladys Olds. *For My Grandchildren: A Picture Book of Some of the Homes of their Ancestors.* Lansing, 1961.

Baker, Henry B. *Lansing Illustrated.* New York, 1888.

Berg, Peter I. "Welfare Capitalism at the REO Motor Car Company," *Michigan History* 69.6 (1985).

Cowles, Albert Eugene. *Past and Present of the City of Lansing and Ingham County, Michigan.* Lansing, 1905.

Edmonds, J.P. *Early Lansing History.* Lansing, 1944.

Flink, James K. *America Adopts the Automobile, 1895-1910.* Cambridge, 1970.

Fine, Lisa M. "Rights of Men, Rites of Passage: Hunting and Masculinity at REO Motors of Lansing, Michigan, 1945–1975." *Journal of Social History,* 33.4 (2000).

Fine, Lisa M. "Our Big Factory Family: Masculinity and Paternalism at the REO Motor Car Company of Lansing, Michigan." *Labor History* 34.2-3 (1993).

Long, John C. *Roy D. Chapin.* Bethlehem, Pa, 1945.

Kestenbaum, Justin. *Out of a Wilderness.* Woodland Hills, Ca, 1981.

Manassah, Sallie M. *Lansing: Capital, Campus, and Cars.* East Lansing, Mi, 1986.

May, George S, ed. *Encyclopedia of American Business History and Biography: The Automotive Industry, 1896-1920.* New York, 1990.

May, George S. *R.E. Olds, Auto Industry Pioneer.* Grand Rapids, 1977.

May, George S. *A Most Unique Machine.* Grand Rapids, 1974.

McConnell, Curt. *The Record Setting Trips: By Auto From Coast to Coast.* Stanford, 2003.

McConnell, Curt. *Coast to Coast By Automobile.* Stanford, 2000.

Niemeyer, Glenn A. *The Automotive Career of Ransom E. Olds.* East Lansing, Mi, 1963.

Yarnell, Duane. *Auto Pioneering; The Remarkable Story of Ransom E. Olds, Father of Oldsmobile and REO.* Lansing, Mi, 1949.

A debt is owed to George S. May and Glen Niemeyer for their foundational work on the automotive career of R.E. Olds. Their research is referenced throughout this book.

Other bibliographic materials of note:
David Pfaff's many booklets on Olds, automotive, and motor-related subjects are available from the R.E. Olds Transportation Museum in Lansing, Michigan. Lansing city directories from the time period (1878–1925) were indispensable, as was the online, full-text version of the *New York Times, 1851–2001* (from ProQuest Information and Learning), *Digital Sanborn Maps, 1867–1970* (also from ProQuest), and the historical backfile of the *Lansing State Journal/Lansing State Republican* (available on microfilm from the Lansing Public Library).